AF252083

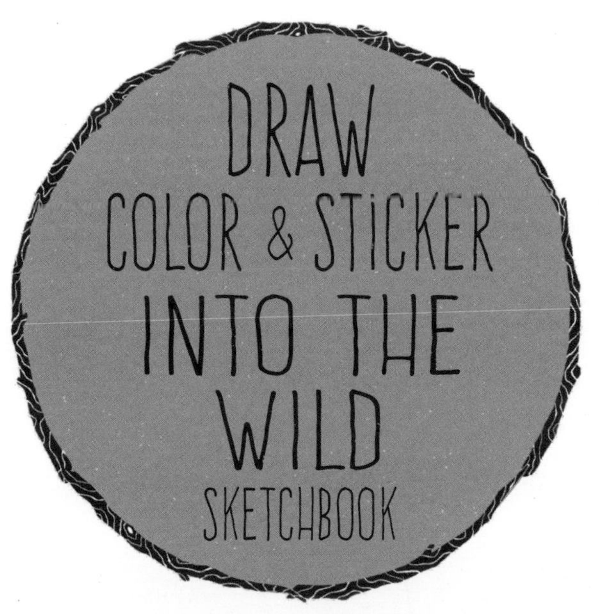

DRAW
COLOR & STICKER
INTO THE
WILD
SKETCHBOOK

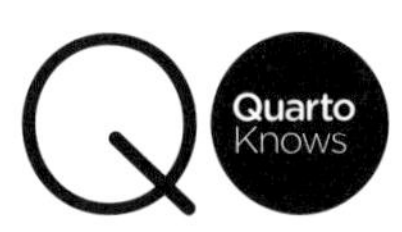

Quarto is the authority on a wide range of topics.

Quarto educates, entertains and enriches the lives of our readers—enthusiasts and lovers of hands-on living.

www.quartoknows.com

© 2017 Quarto Publishing Group USA Inc.
Illustrations © 2017 Marisa Redondo

First published in the United States of America in 2017 by
Quarry Books, an imprint of
Quarto Publishing Group USA Inc.
100 Cummings Center
Suite 265-D
Beverly, Massachusetts 01915-6101
Telephone: (978) 282-9590
Fax: (978) 283-2742
QuartoKnows.com
Visit our blogs at QuartoKnows.com

All rights reserved. No part of this book may be reproduced in any form without written permission of the copyright owners. All images in this book have been reproduced with the knowledge and prior consent of the artists concerned, and no responsibility is accepted by producer, publisher, or printer for any infringement of copyright or otherwise, arising from the contents of this publication. Every effort has been made to trace the copyright holders and ensure that credits accurately comply with information supplied. We apologize for any inaccuracies that may have occurred and will resolve inaccurate or missing information in a subsequent reprinting of the book.

10 9 8 7 6 5 4 3 2 1

ISBN: 978-1-63159-302-4

Cover Image: Marisa Redondo
Design and Page Layout: Megan Jones Design
Illustration: Marisa Redondo

Printed in China

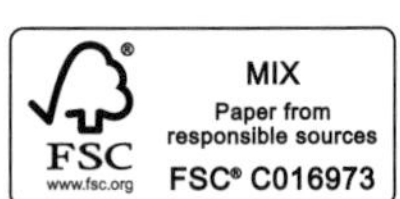

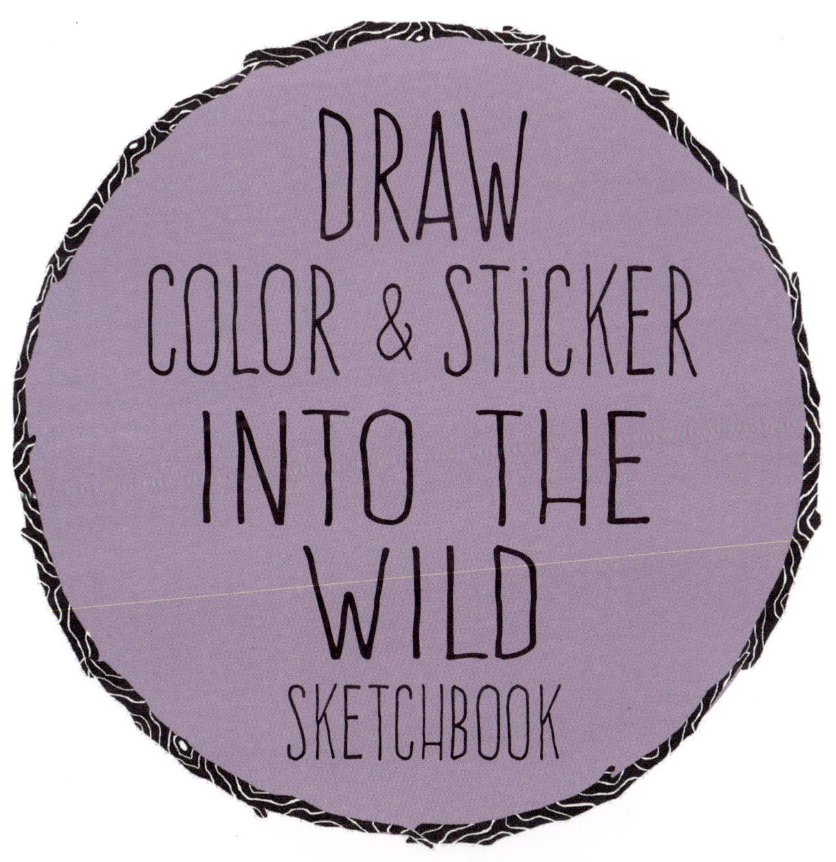

AN IMAGINATIVE ILLUSTRATION JOURNAL

★ *Marisa Redondo* ★

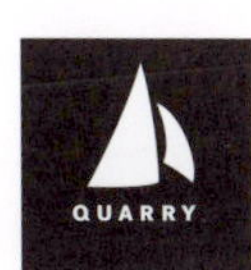

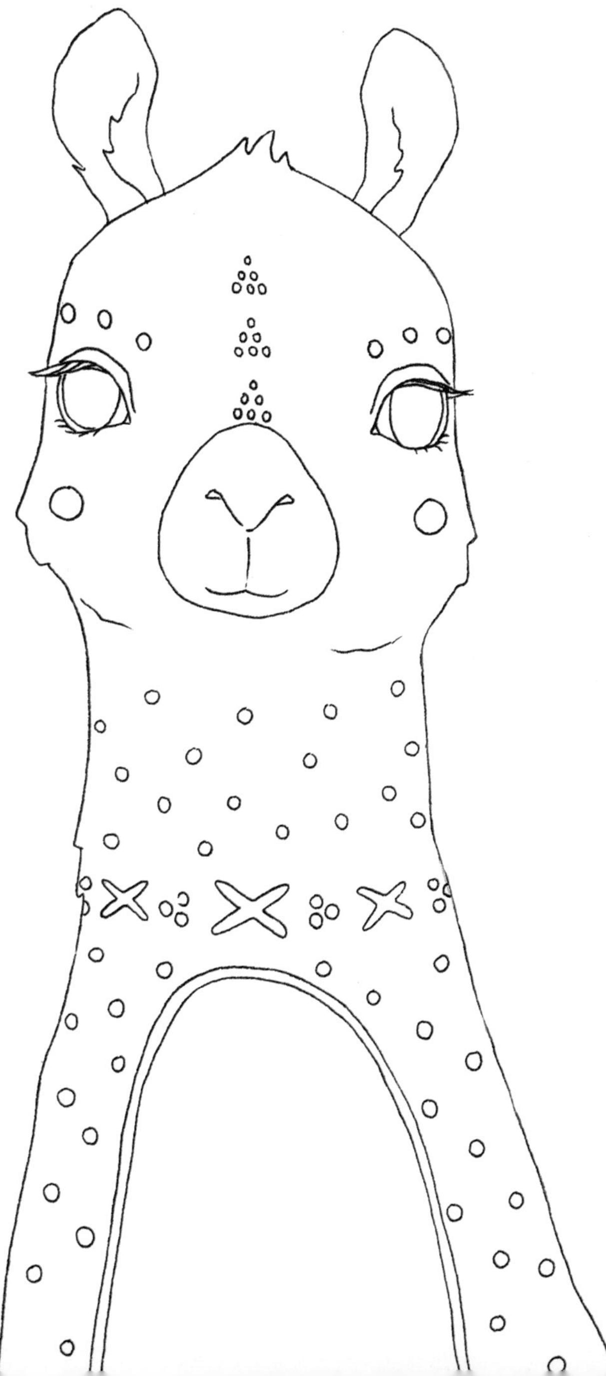

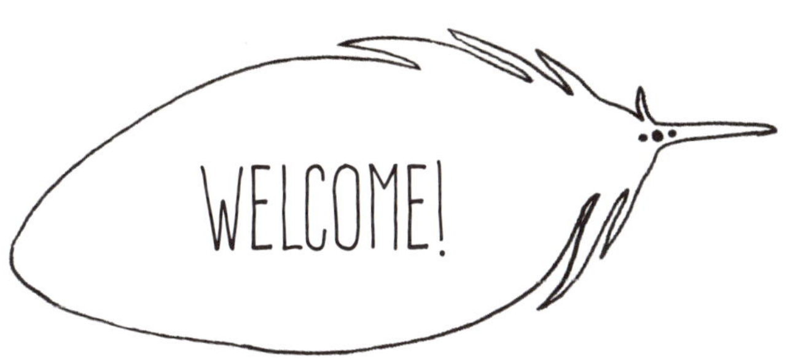

HOW TO USE THIS BOOK

THE NATURE-INSPIRED DESIGNS FEATURED IN THIS BOOK ARE SET UP IN PAIRS. THE FIRST TWO PAGES CONTAIN A FULL DRAWING OF WILDLIFE SCENES AND WOODLAND CREATURES, READY TO COLOR WITH CRAYONS, COLORED PENCILS, MARKERS, OR EVEN WITH WATERCOLORS. IF YOU'RE FEELING ADVENTUROUS, DRAW IN A FEW EXTRA DETAILS OF YOUR OWN WITH A PERMANENT MARKER. THE NEXT TWO PAGES IN THE PAIR CONTINUE THE THEME WITH A PARTIAL DRAWING FOR YOU TO COMPLETE. USE THE AUTHOR'S FINISHED DRAWING AS INSPIRATION, OR LET YOUR IMAGINATION GUIDE YOUR HAND AS YOU DOODLE YOUR WAY TO A FANCIFUL SCENE. A FINE-LINE, BLACK PERMANENT MARKER WILL COMPLEMENT THE ORIGINAL DRAWING, BUT FEEL FREE TO USE ANY TOOLS AND COLORS THAT APPEAL TO YOU. IN THE BACK OF THE BOOK, YOU'LL FIND A COORDINATING STICKER PAGE FOR EACH DESIGN THEME, PLUS TWO EXTRA STICKER PAGES THAT CAN BE USED ANYWHERE. COLOR IN THE STICKERS OR ADD HAND-DRAWN EMBELLISHMENTS TO MAKE EACH ONE UNIQUELY YOUR OWN. ENHANCE THE THEME PAGES WITH THEIR CORRESPONDING STICKERS, OR MIX AND MATCH THE STICKERS THROUGHOUT THE BOOK TO CREATE FUN DESIGNS IN YOUR OWN VISION.

FOLLOW THE PROMPTS ON EACH PAGE AS YOU DRAW, COLOR, AND STICKER YOUR WAY THROUGH THIS BOOK. MOST IMPORTANTLY, HAVE FUN, AND TAKE CREATIVE CHANCES! THE RESULTS MAY SURPRISE YOU.

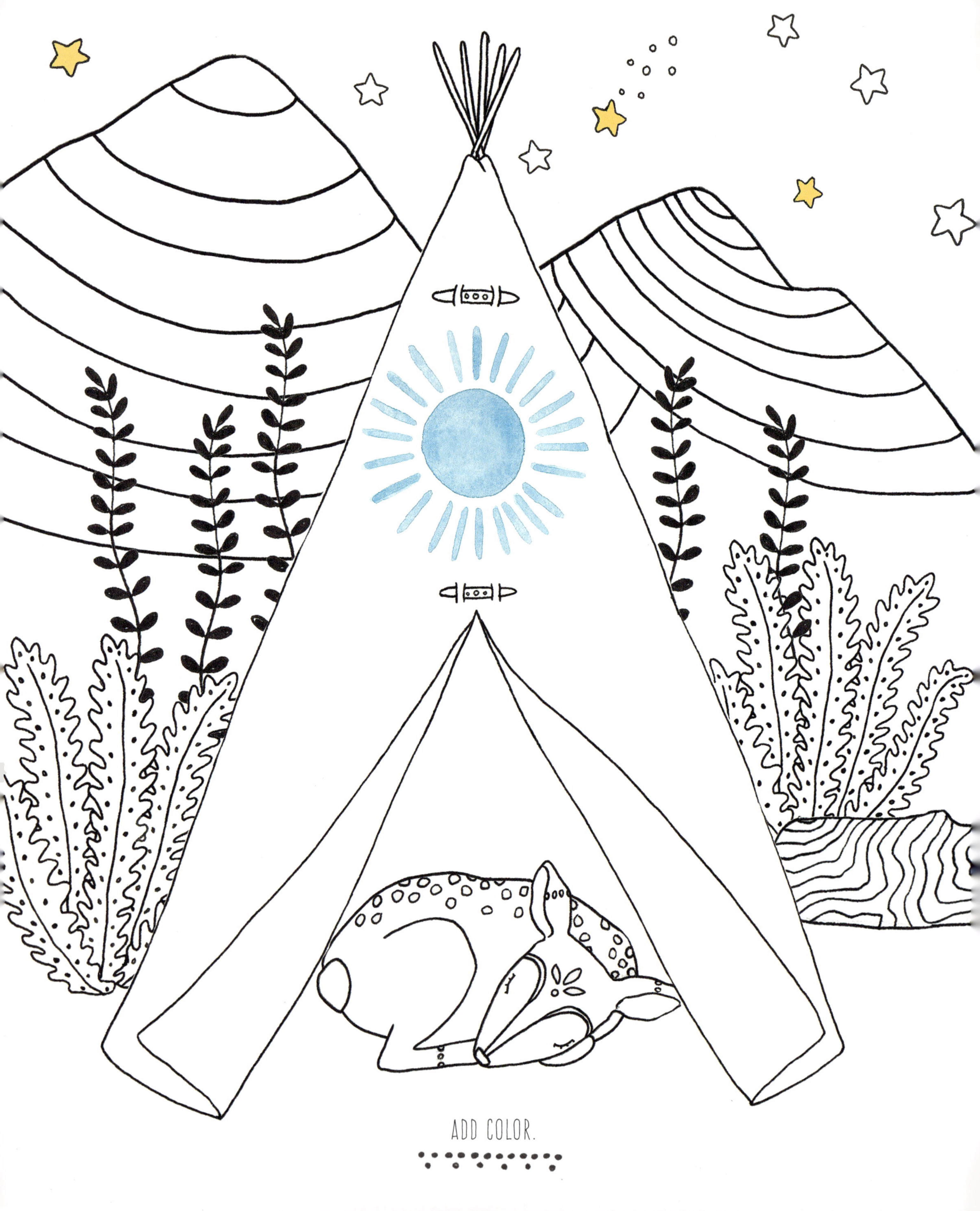

ADD COLOR.

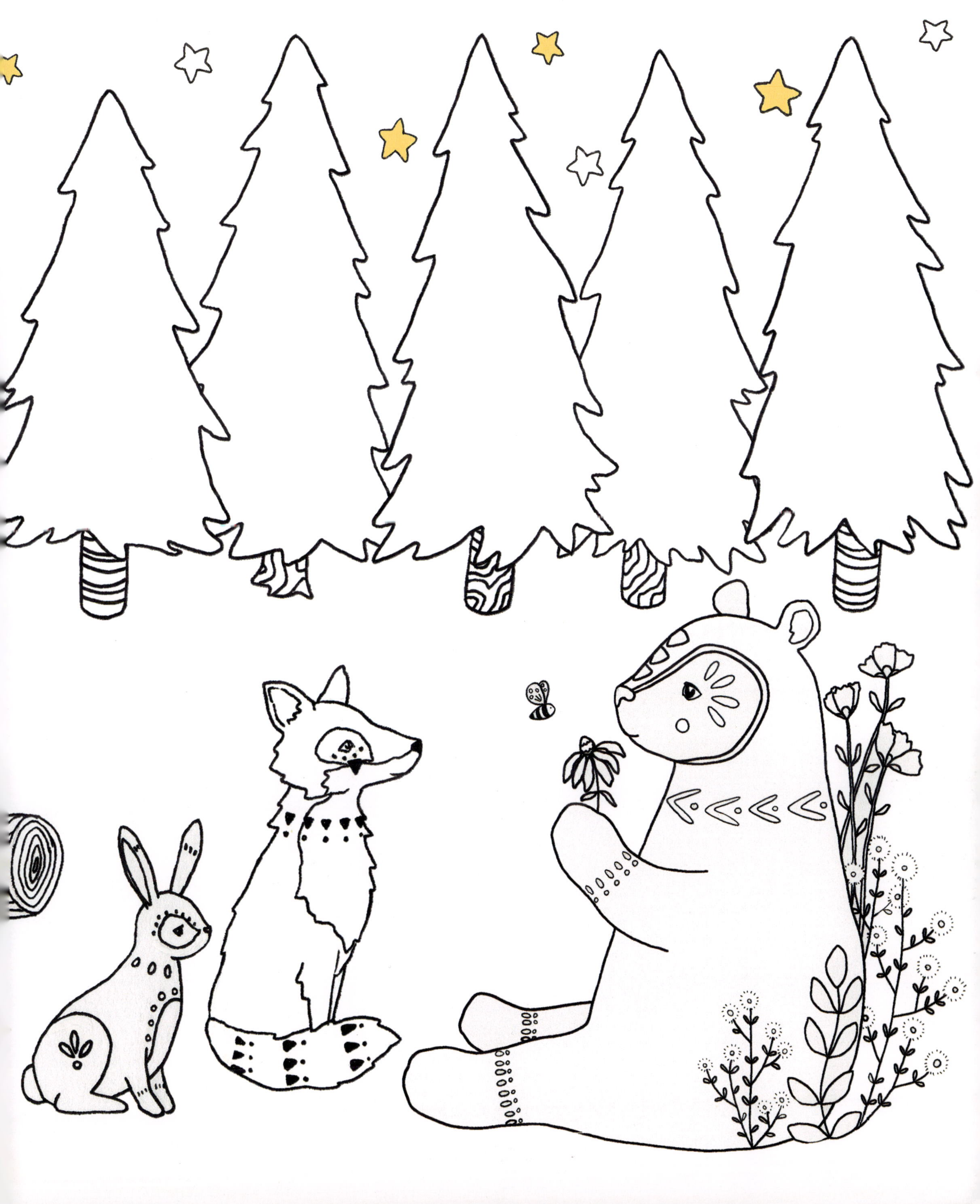

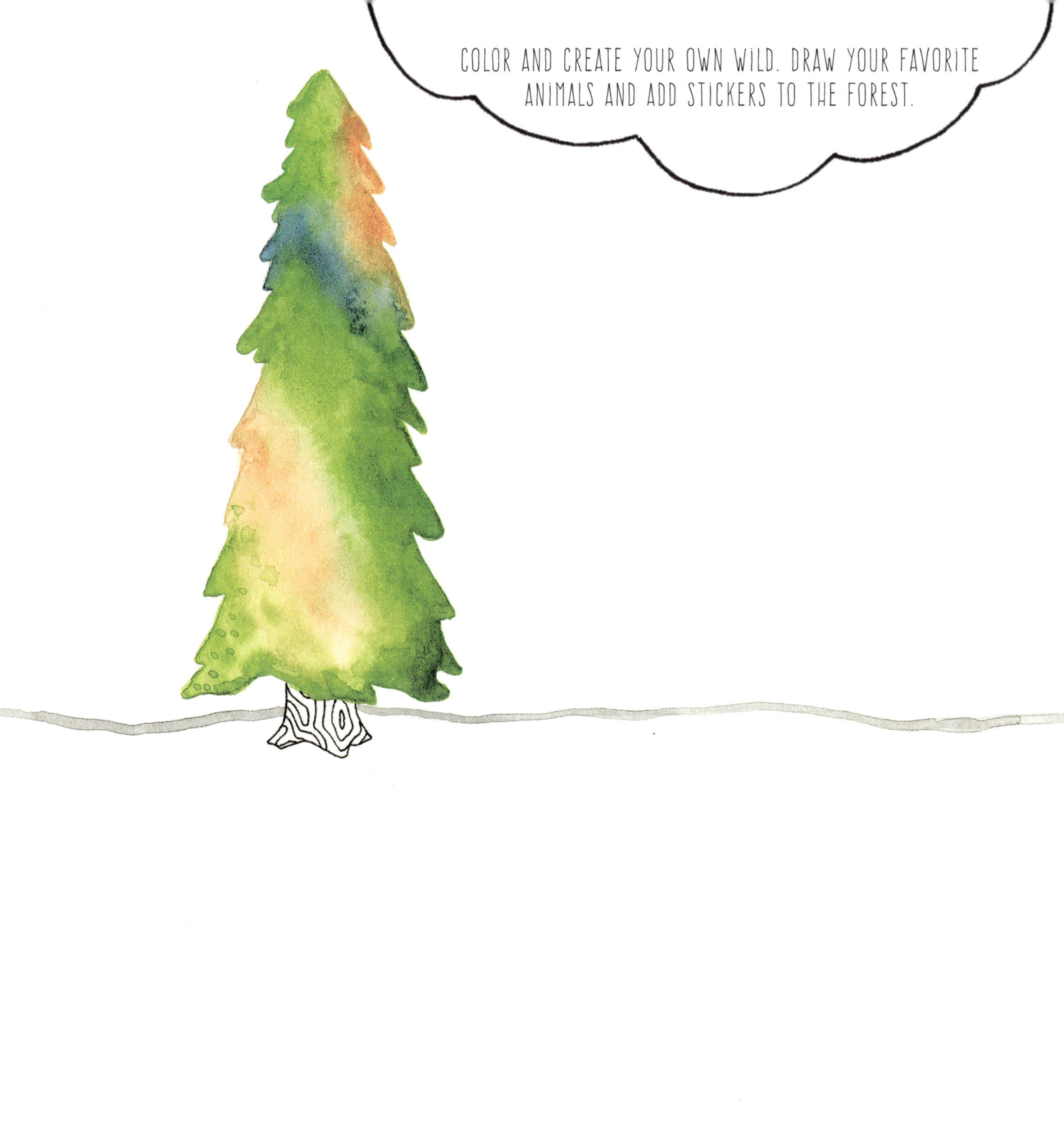

COLOR AND CREATE YOUR OWN WILD. DRAW YOUR FAVORITE
ANIMALS AND ADD STICKERS TO THE FOREST.

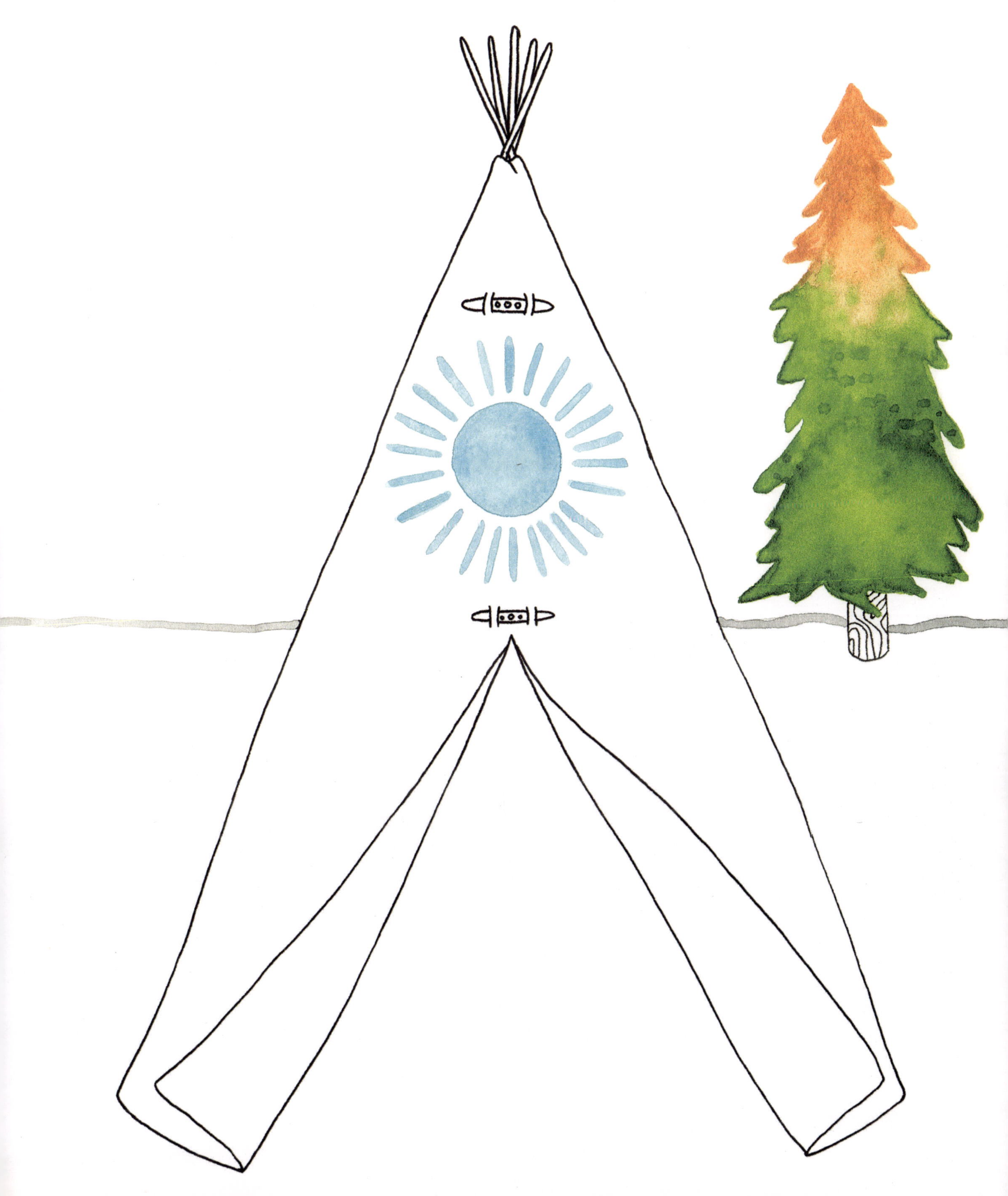

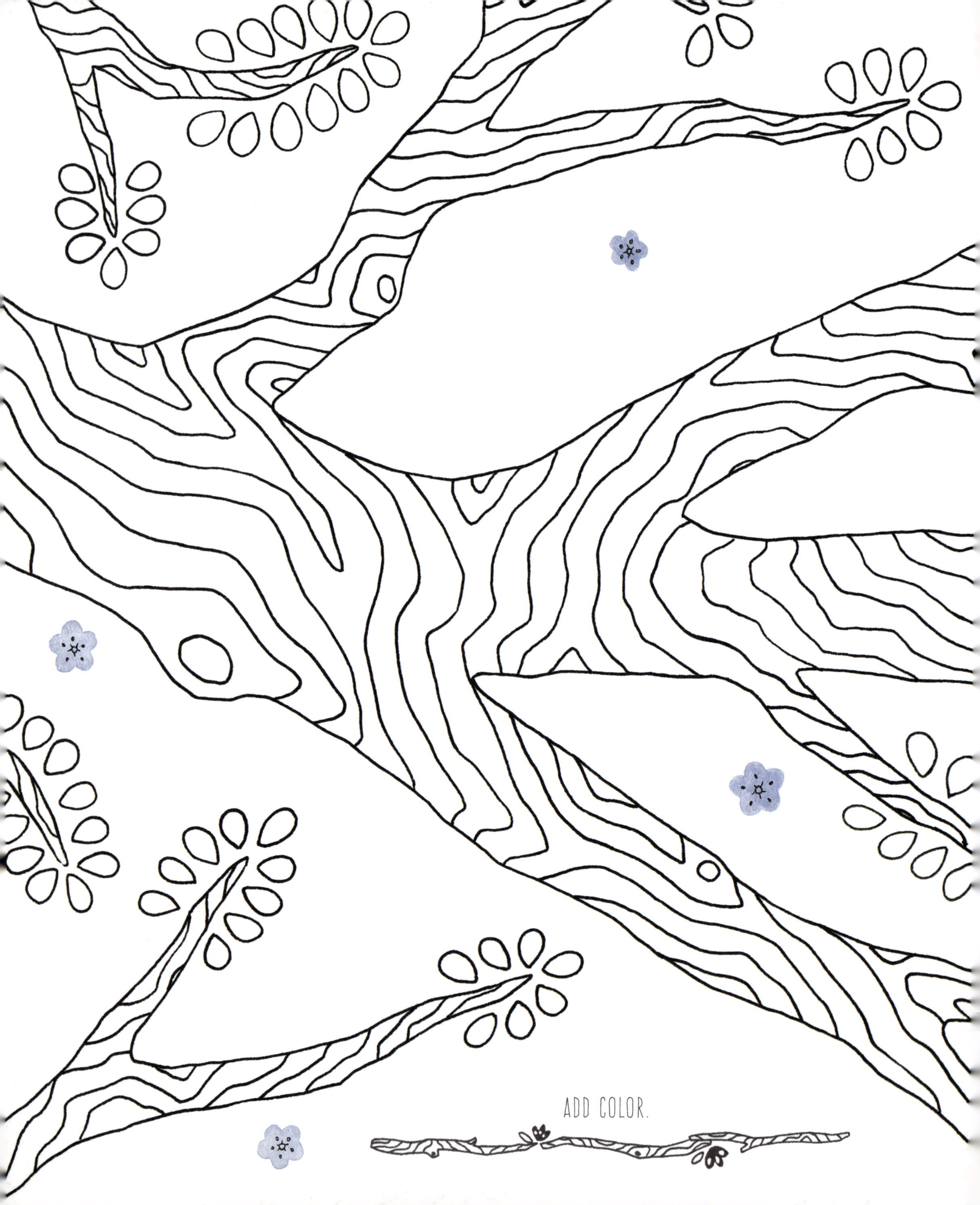

ADD COLOR.

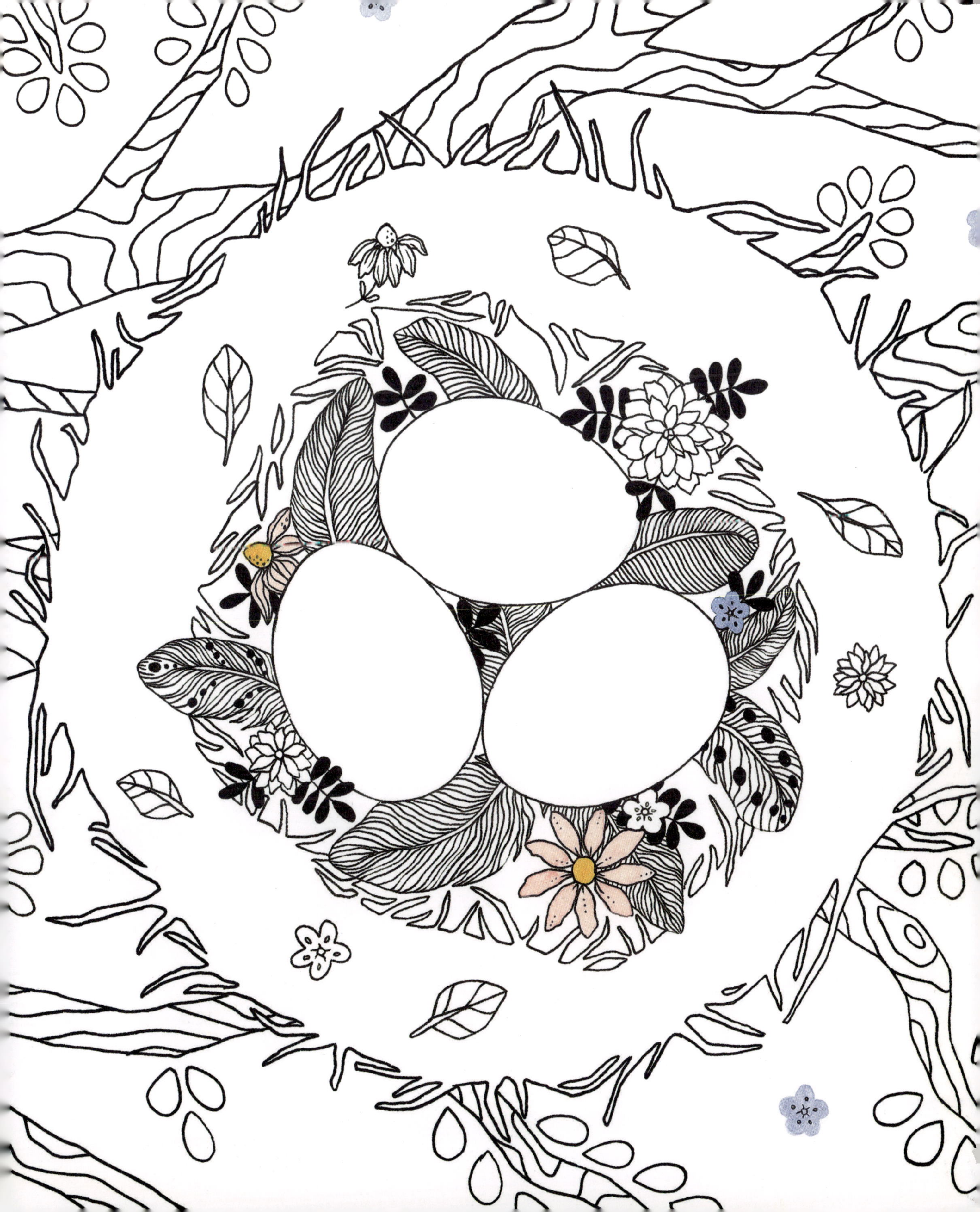

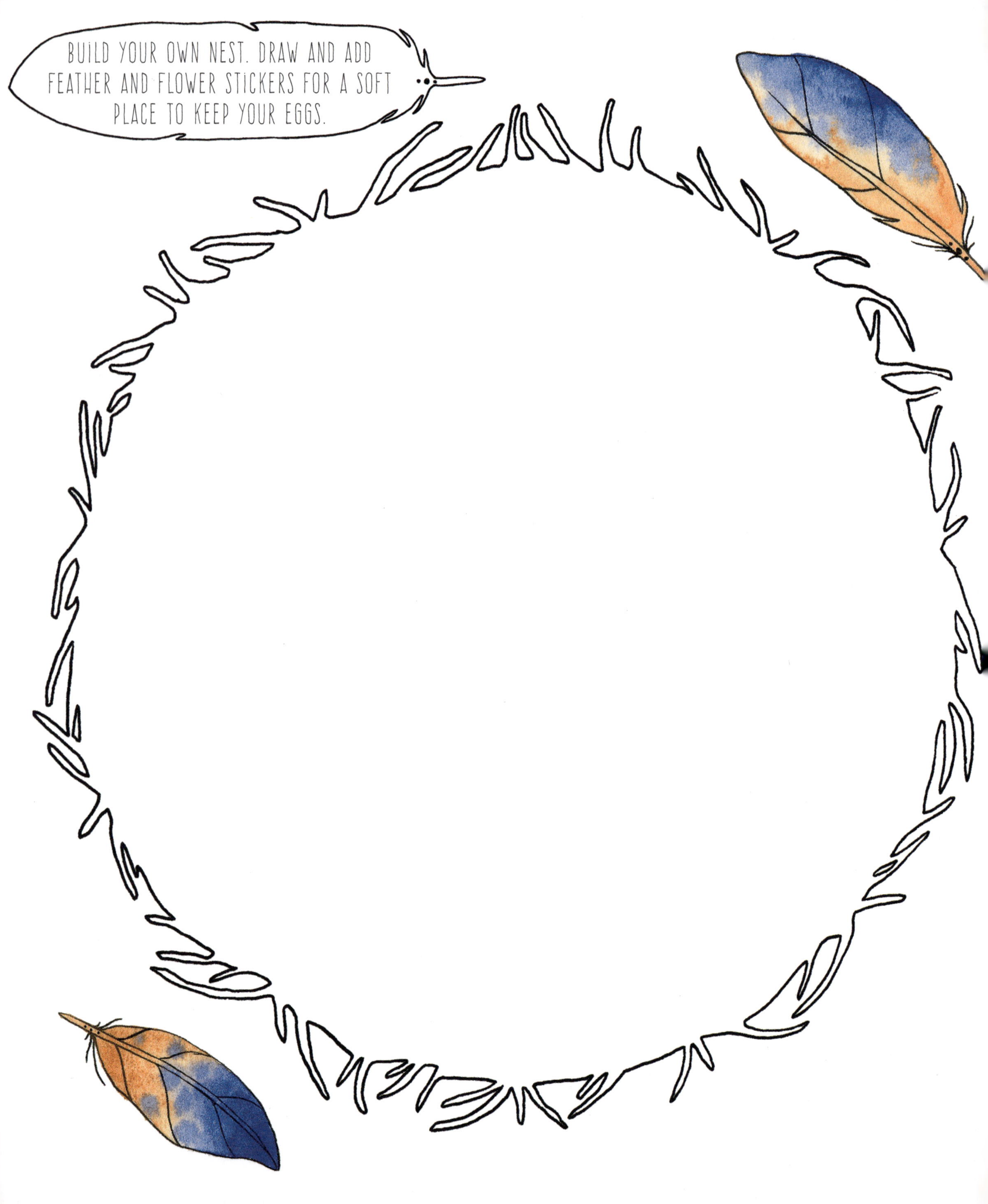

BUILD YOUR OWN NEST. DRAW AND ADD
FEATHER AND FLOWER STICKERS FOR A SOFT
PLACE TO KEEP YOUR EGGS.

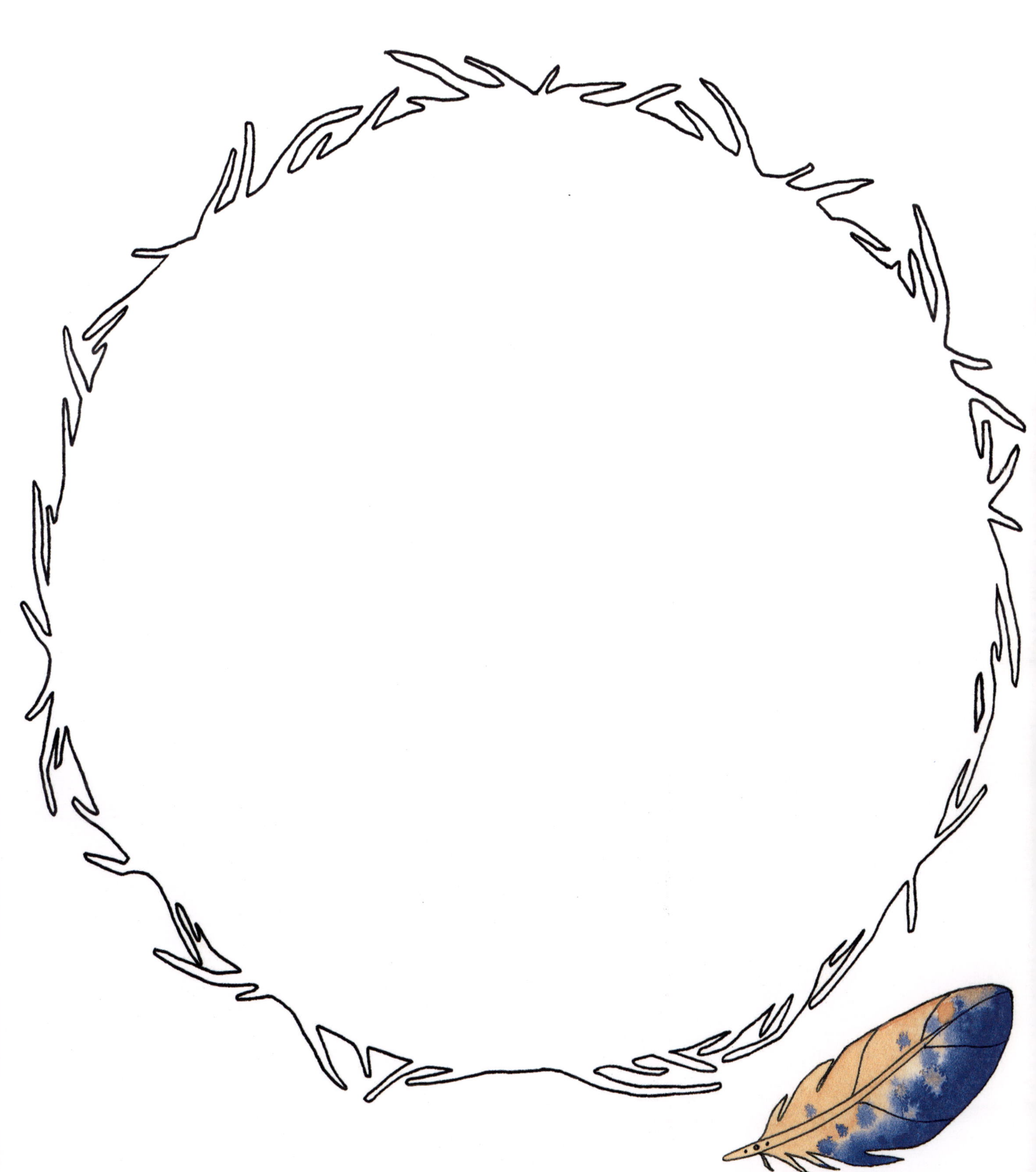

ADD COLOR.

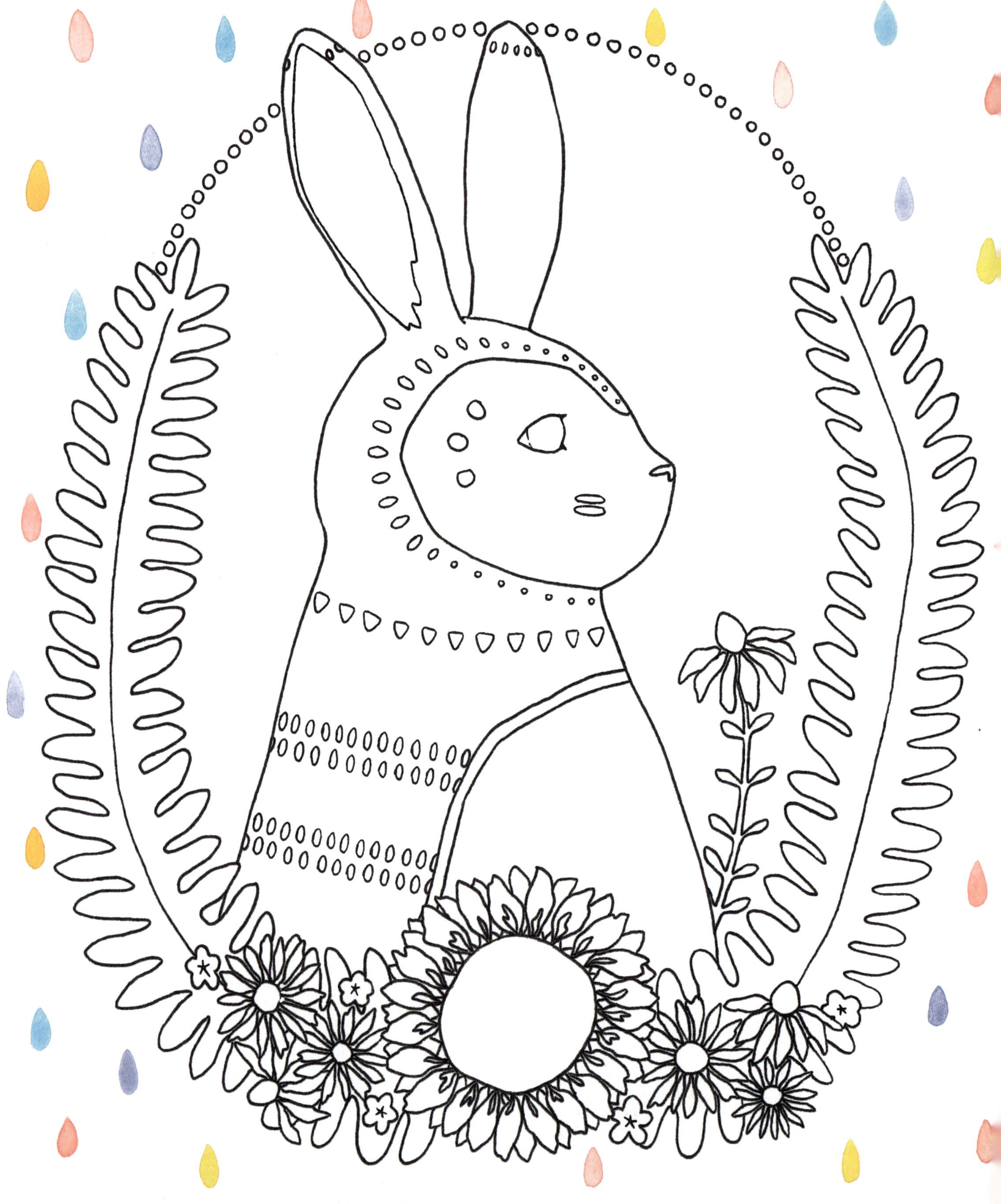

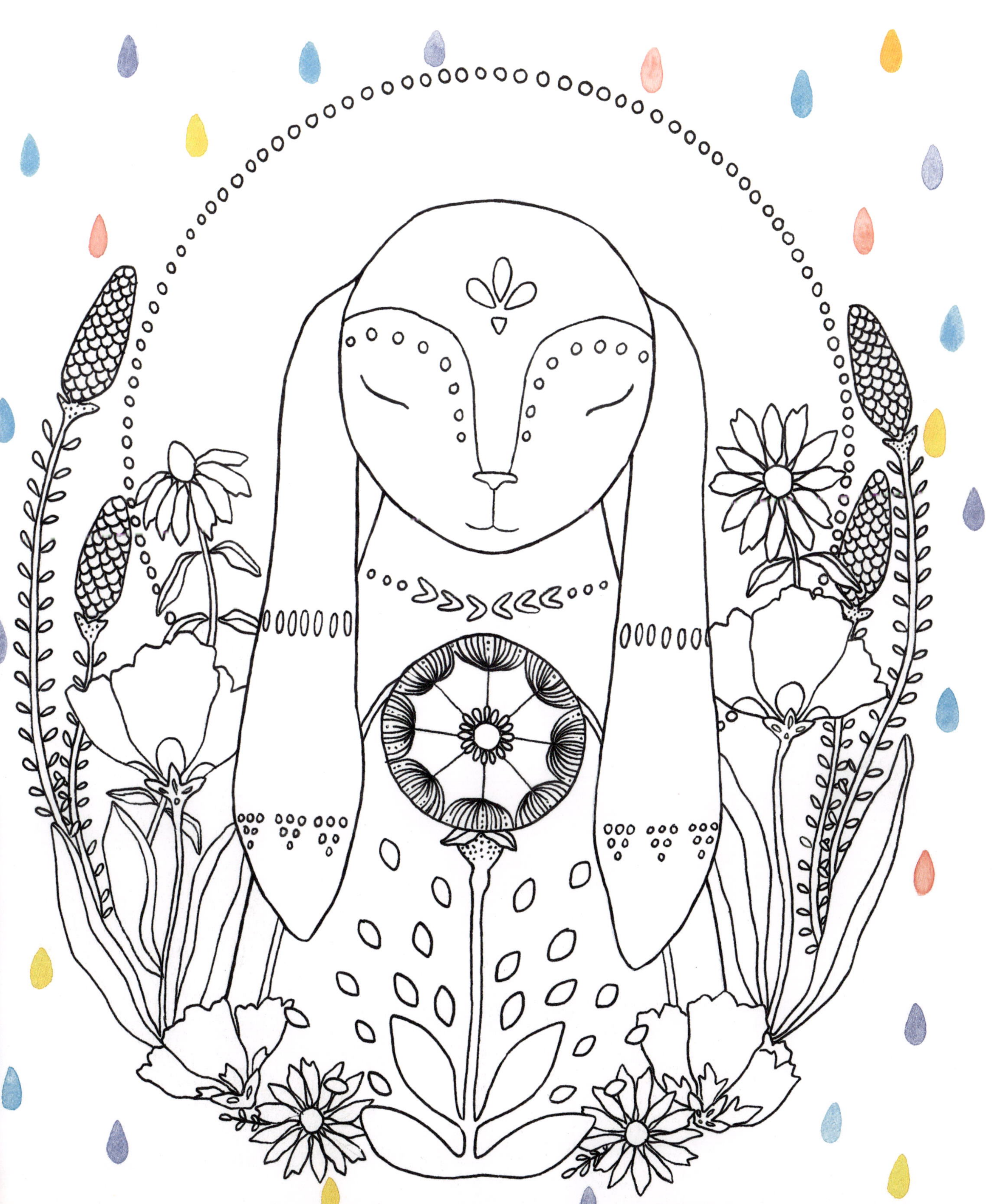

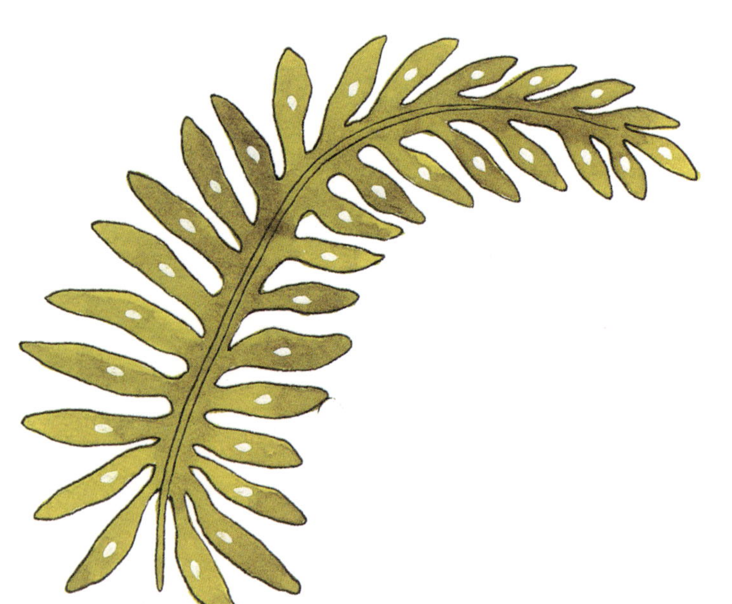

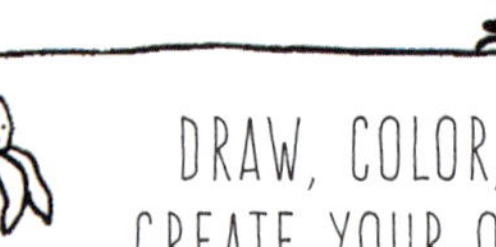

DRAW, COLOR, AND ADD STICKERS TO
CREATE YOUR OWN BUNNY MEADOW. ADD
YOUR FAVORITE FLOWERS AND PLANTS.

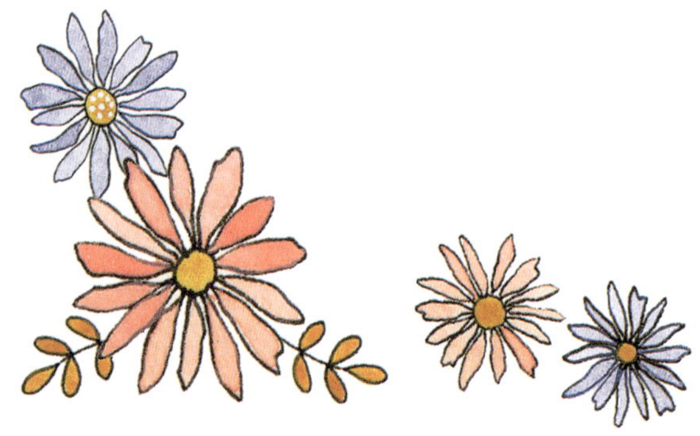

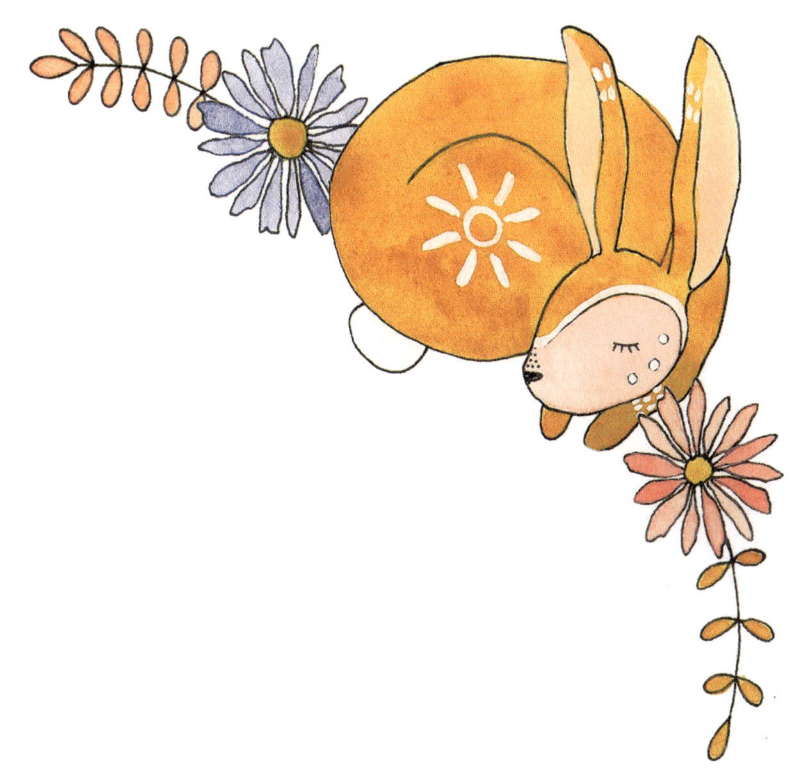
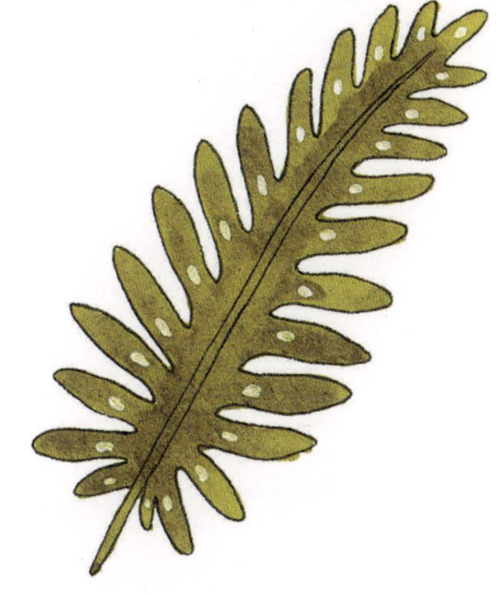

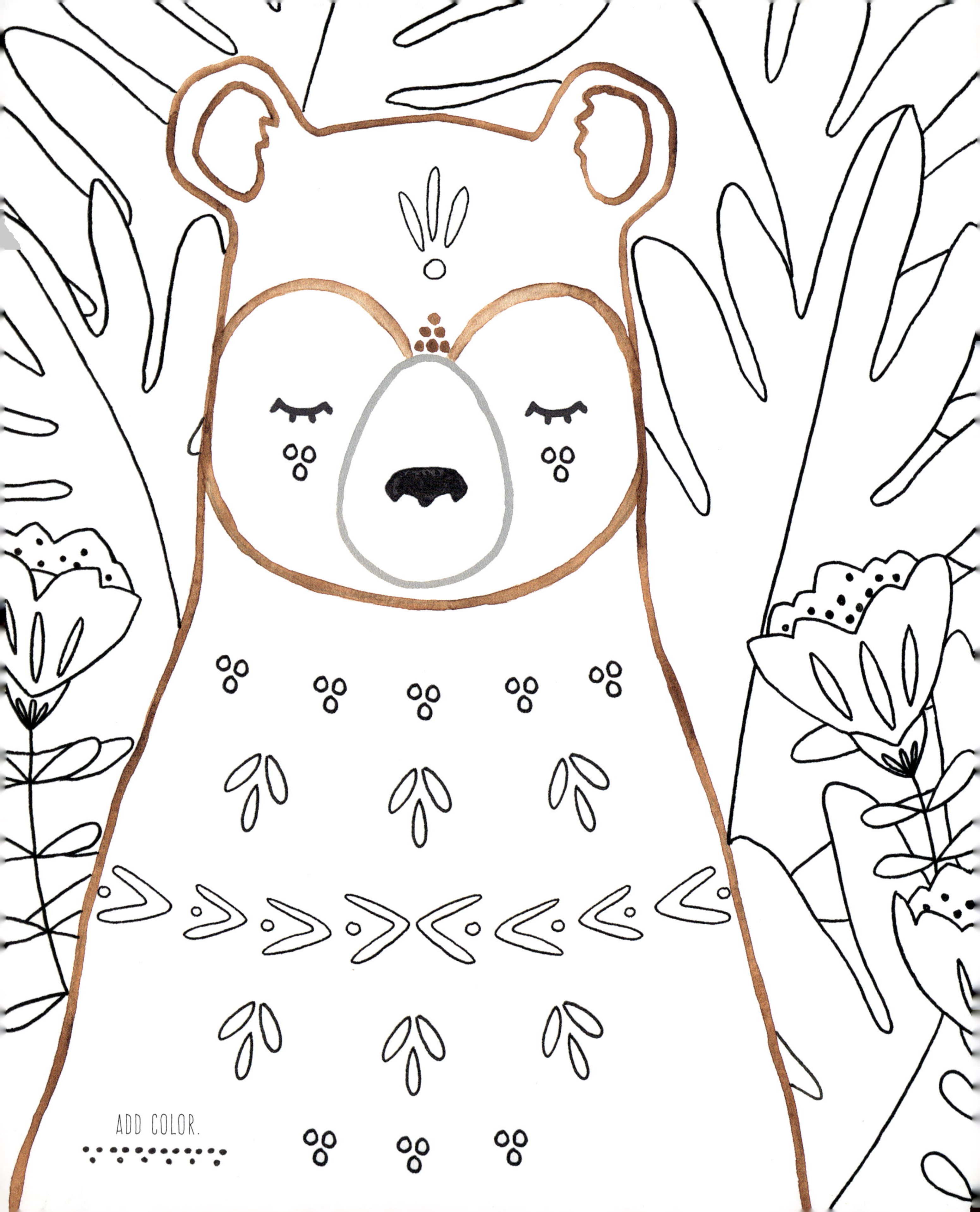
ADD COLOR.

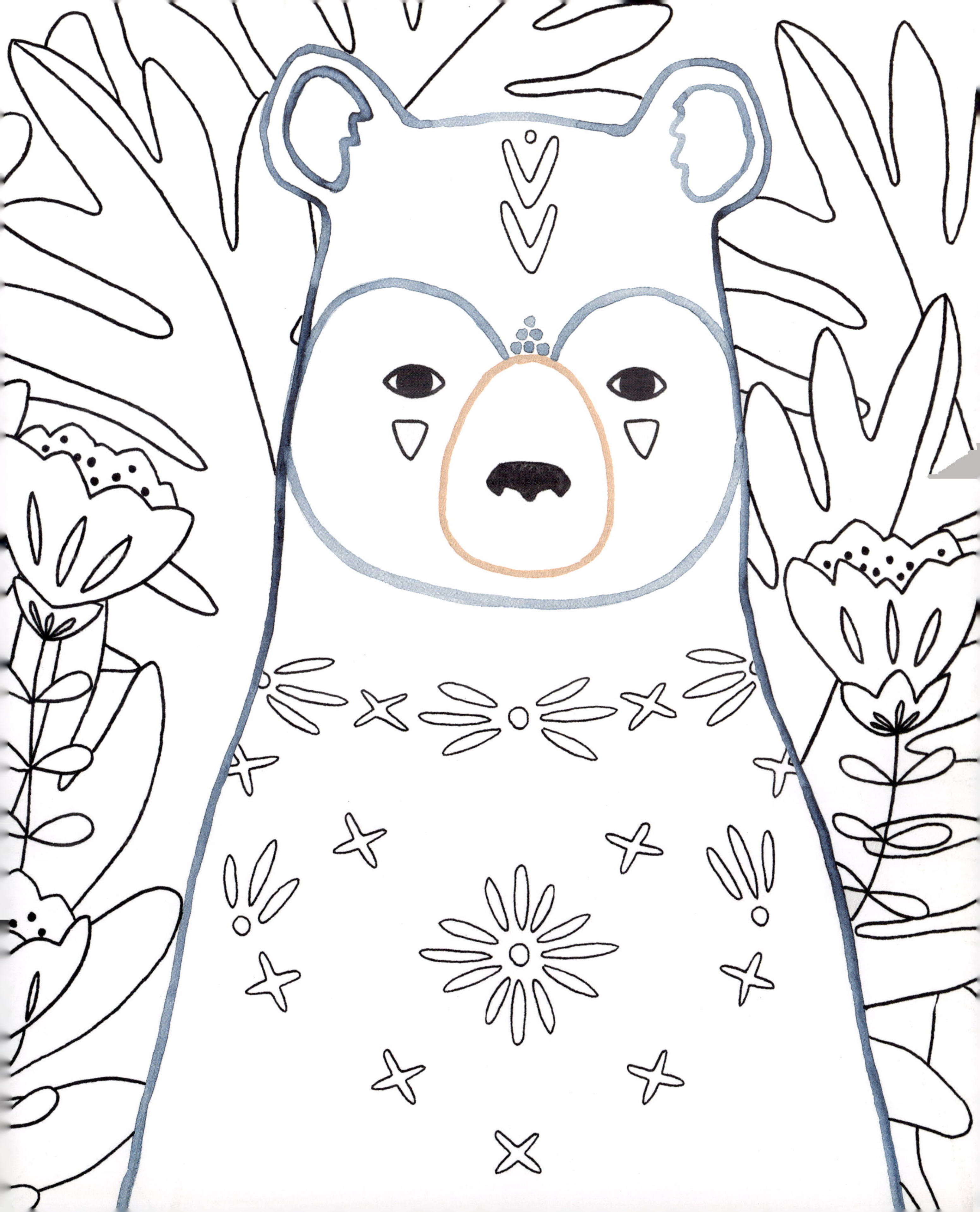

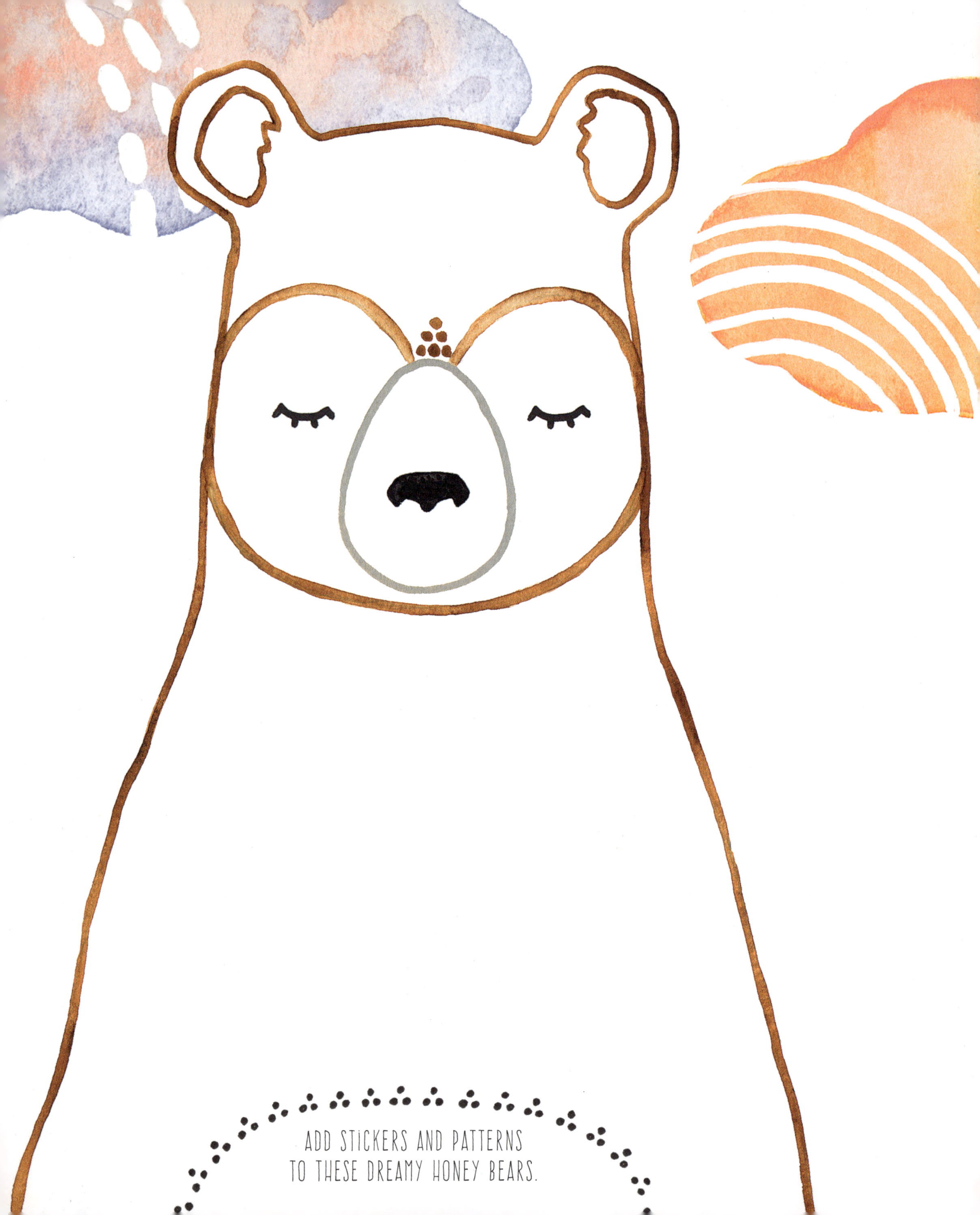

ADD STICKERS AND PATTERNS
TO THESE DREAMY HONEY BEARS.

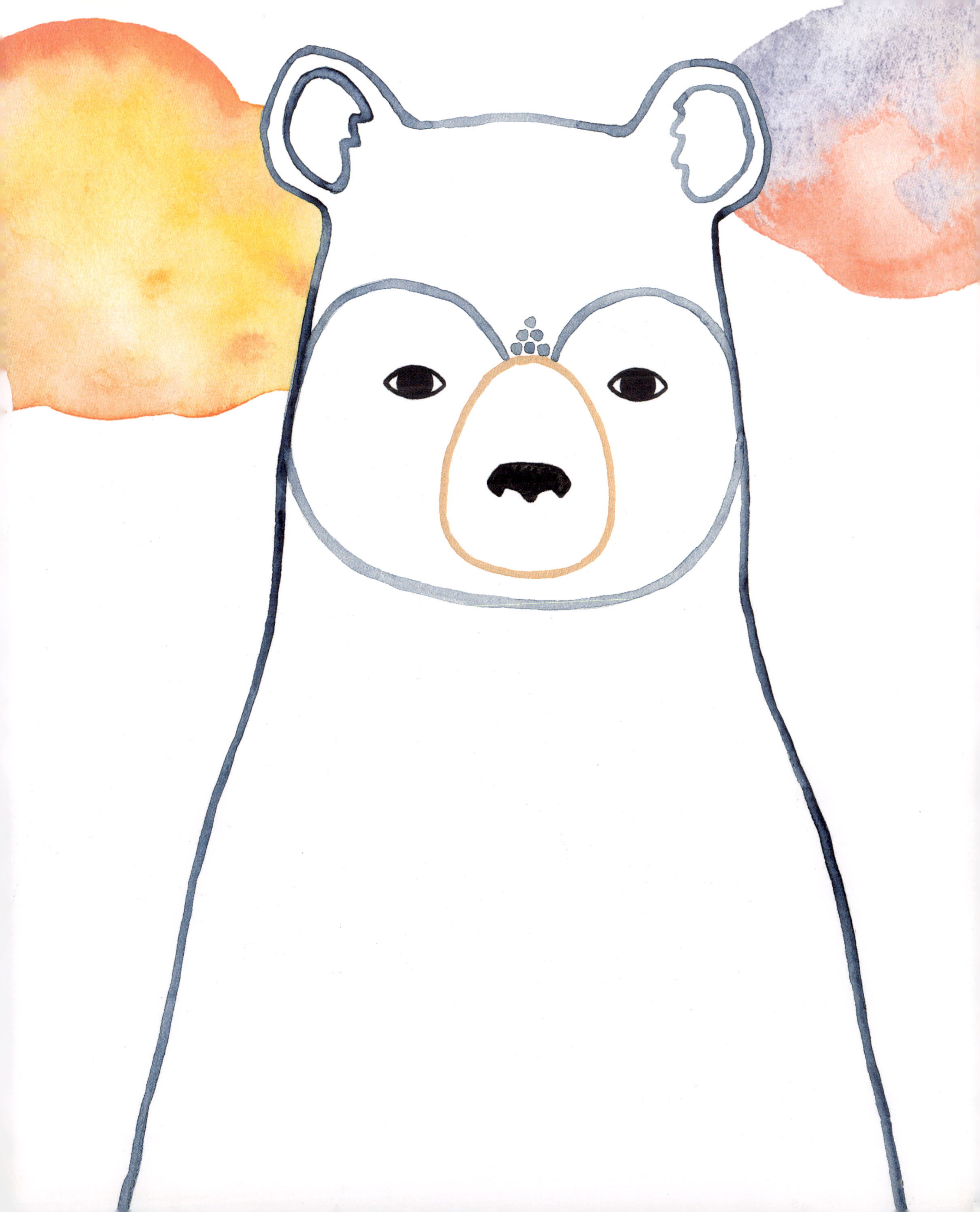

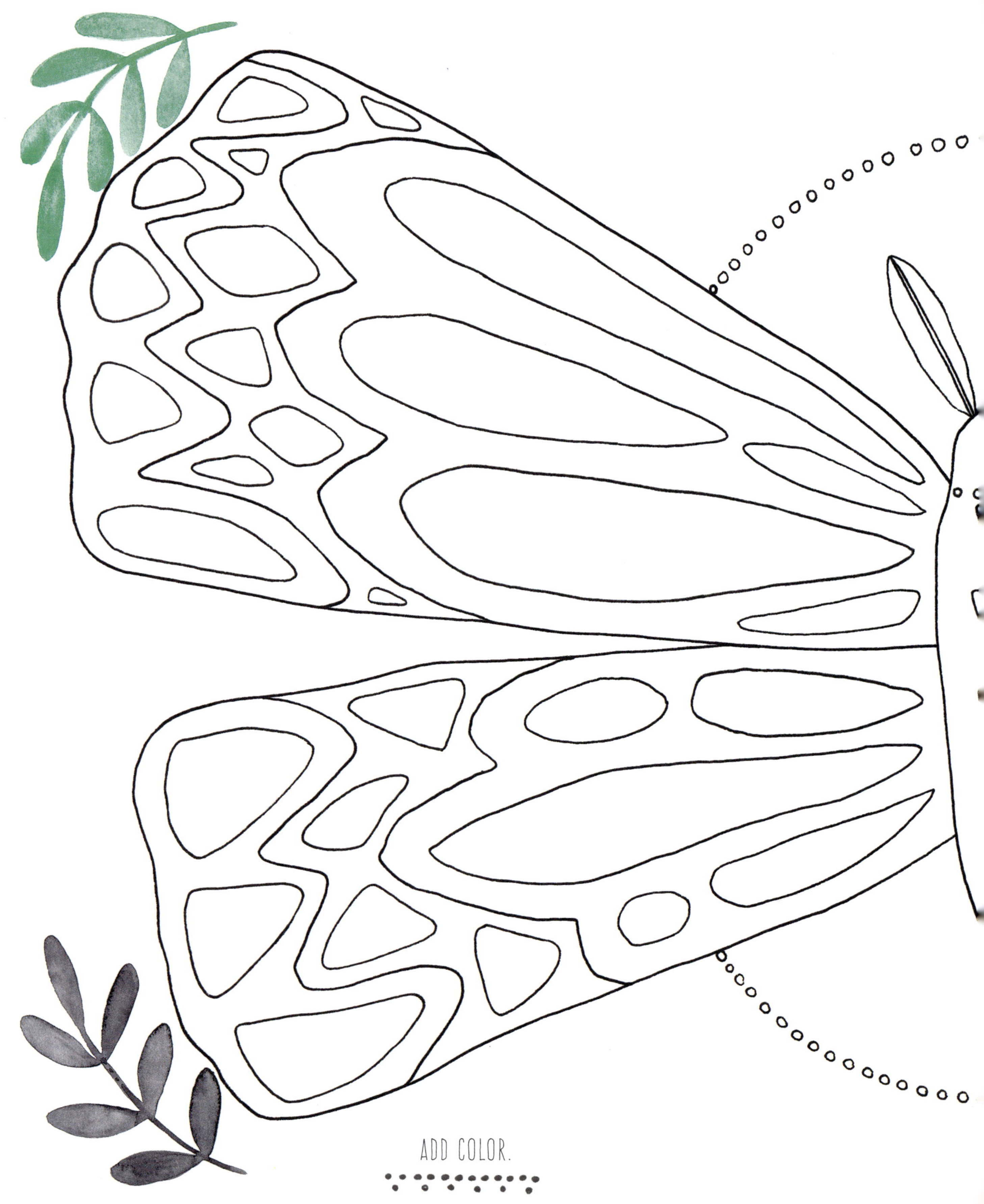

ADD COLOR.

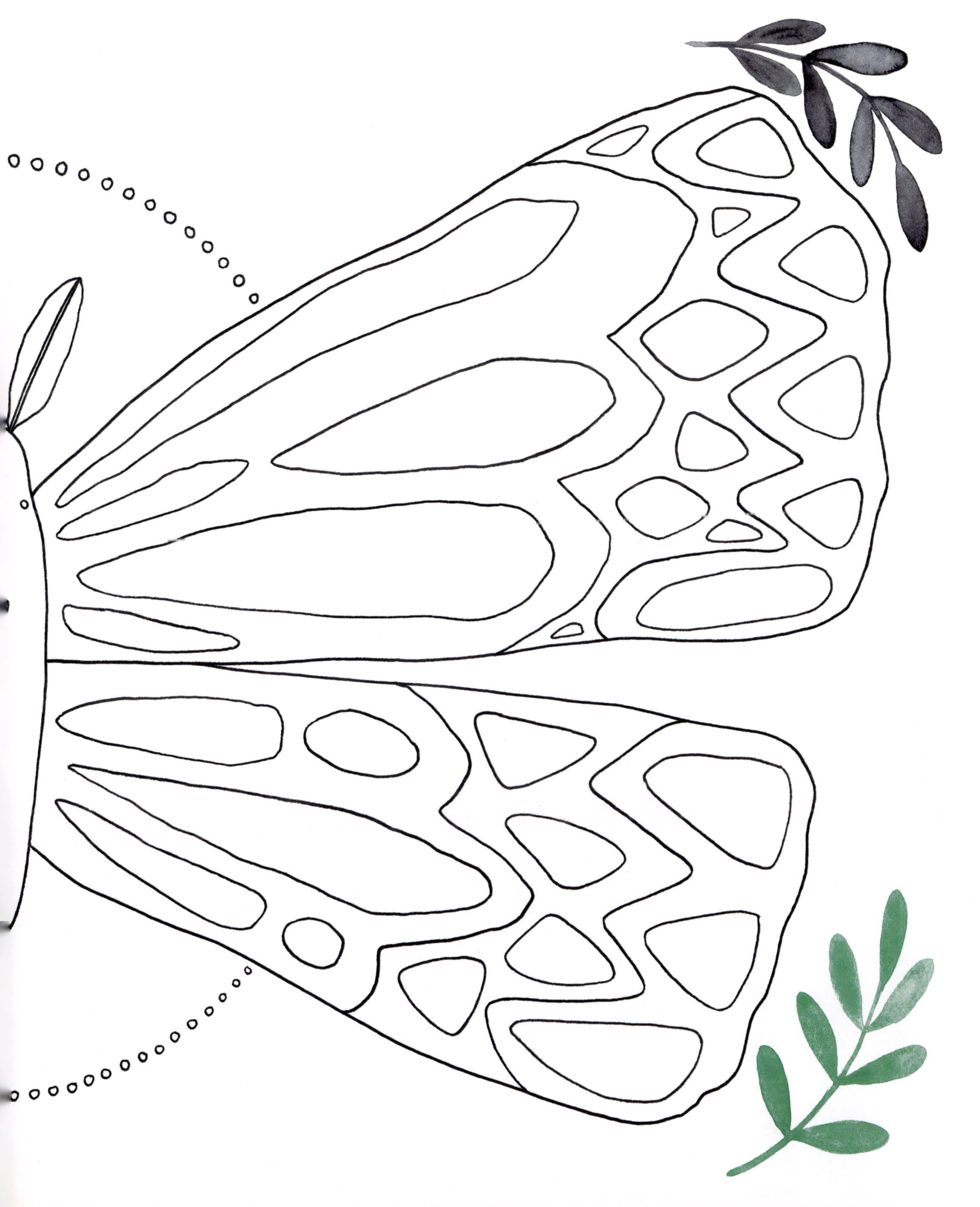

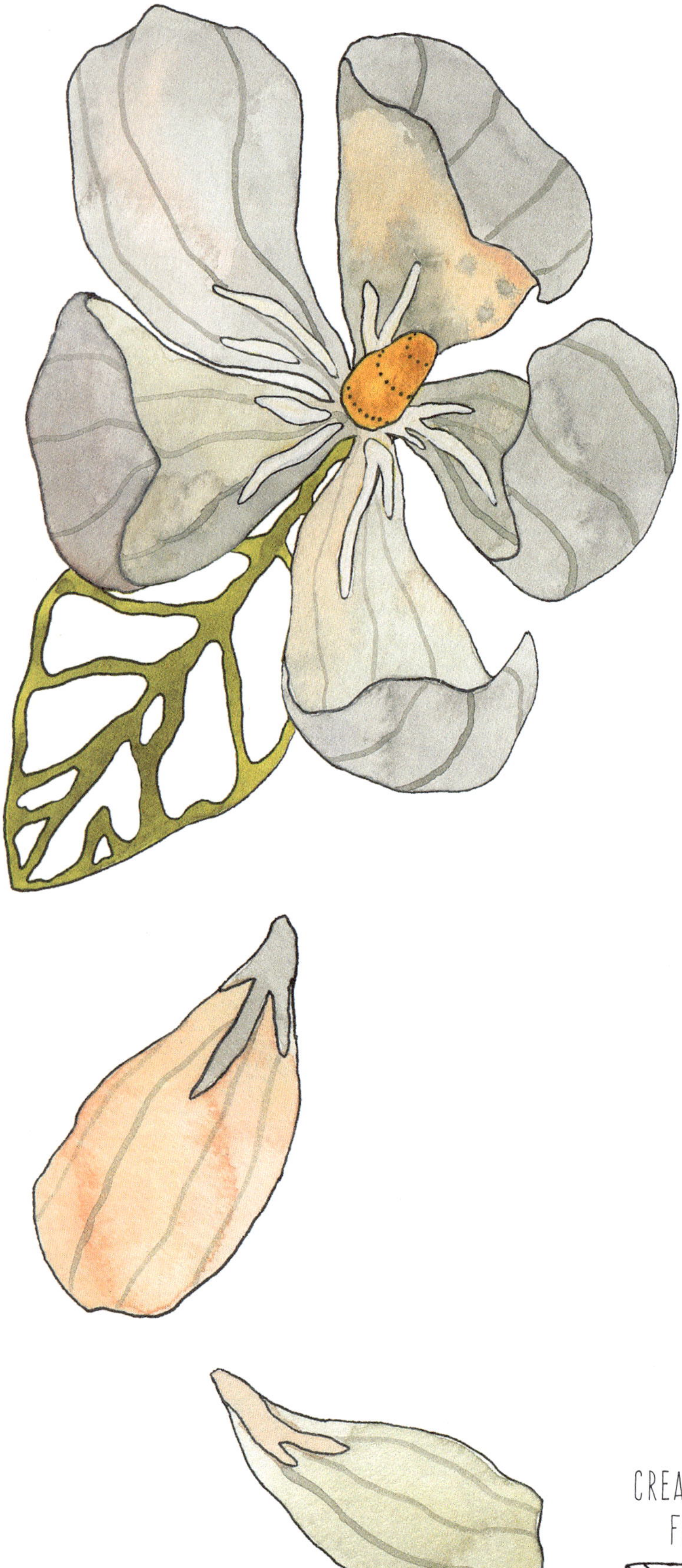

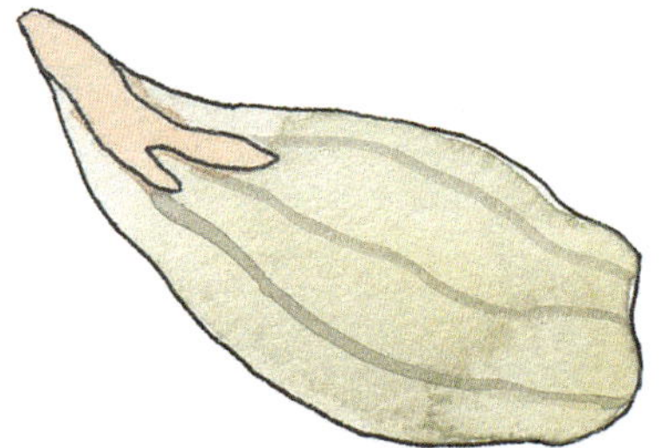

CREATE A COLORFUL ENVIRONMENT AND DRAW FLOWERS
FOR YOUR BUTTERFLIES TO DRINK NECTAR FROM.

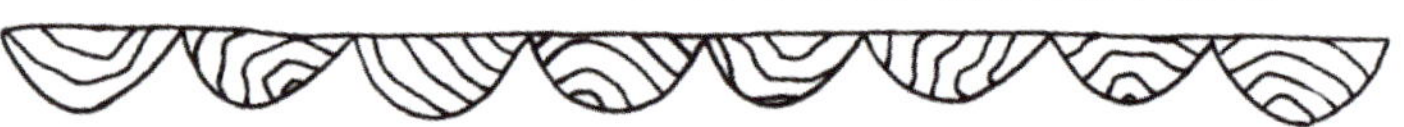

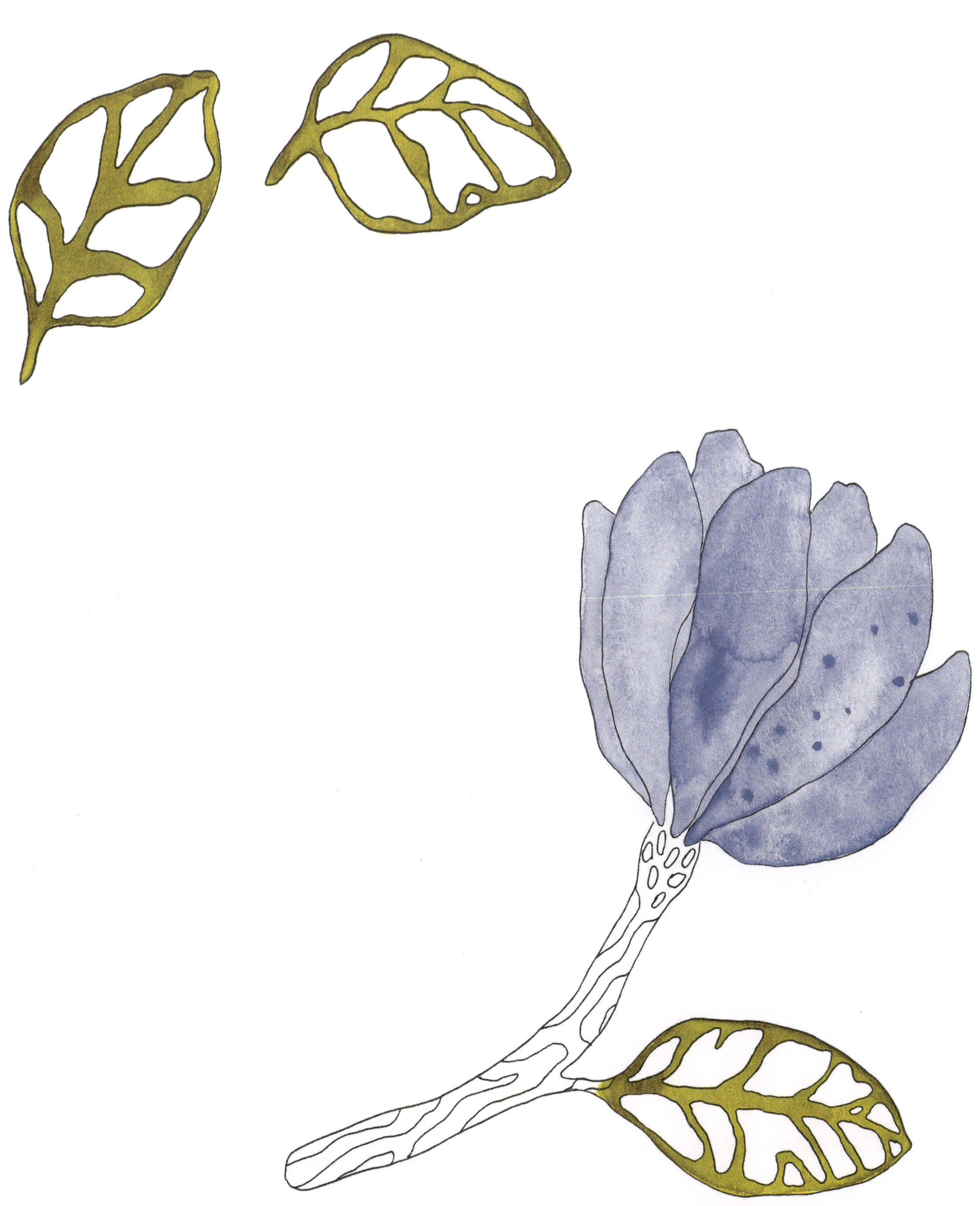

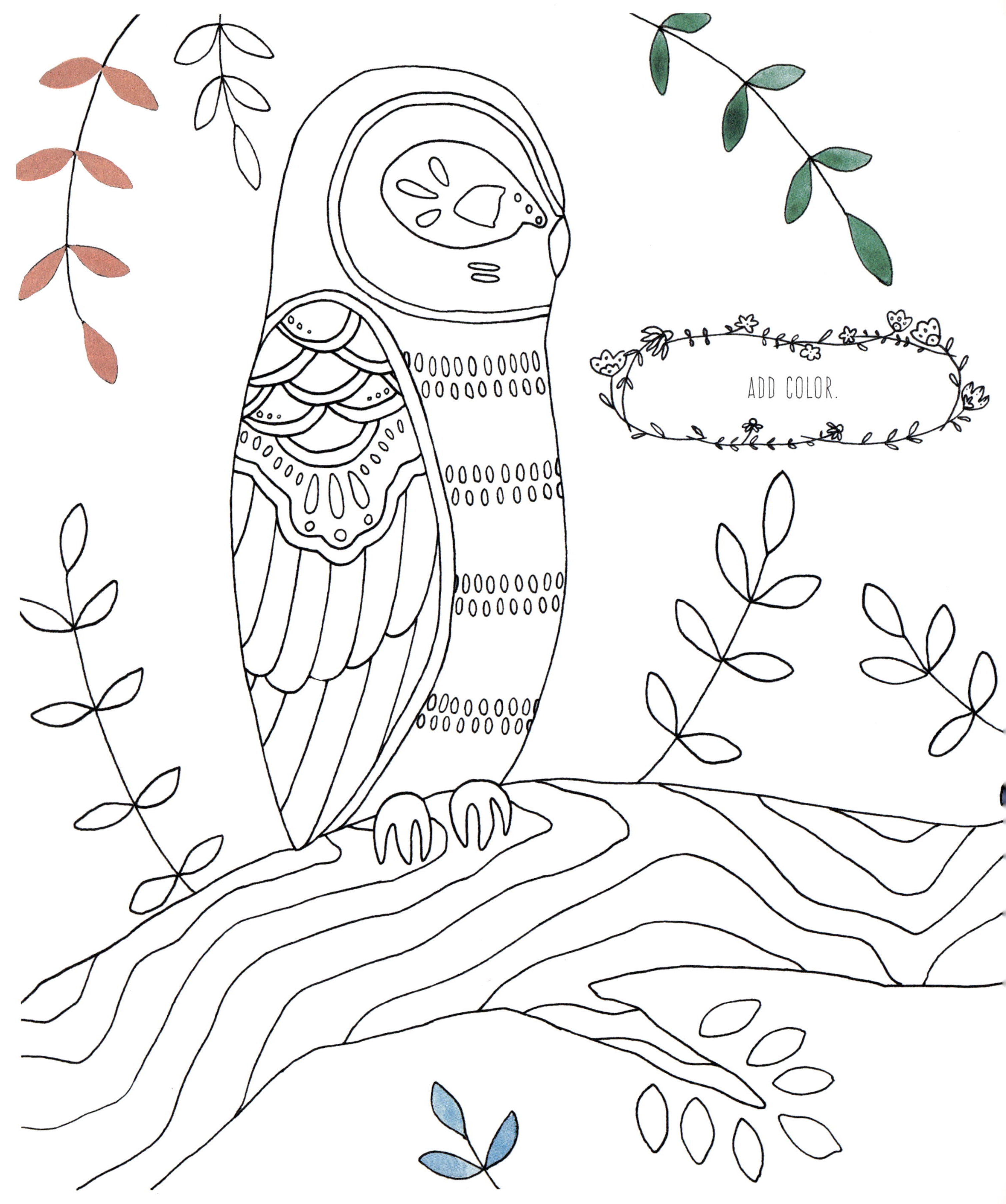
ADD COLOR.

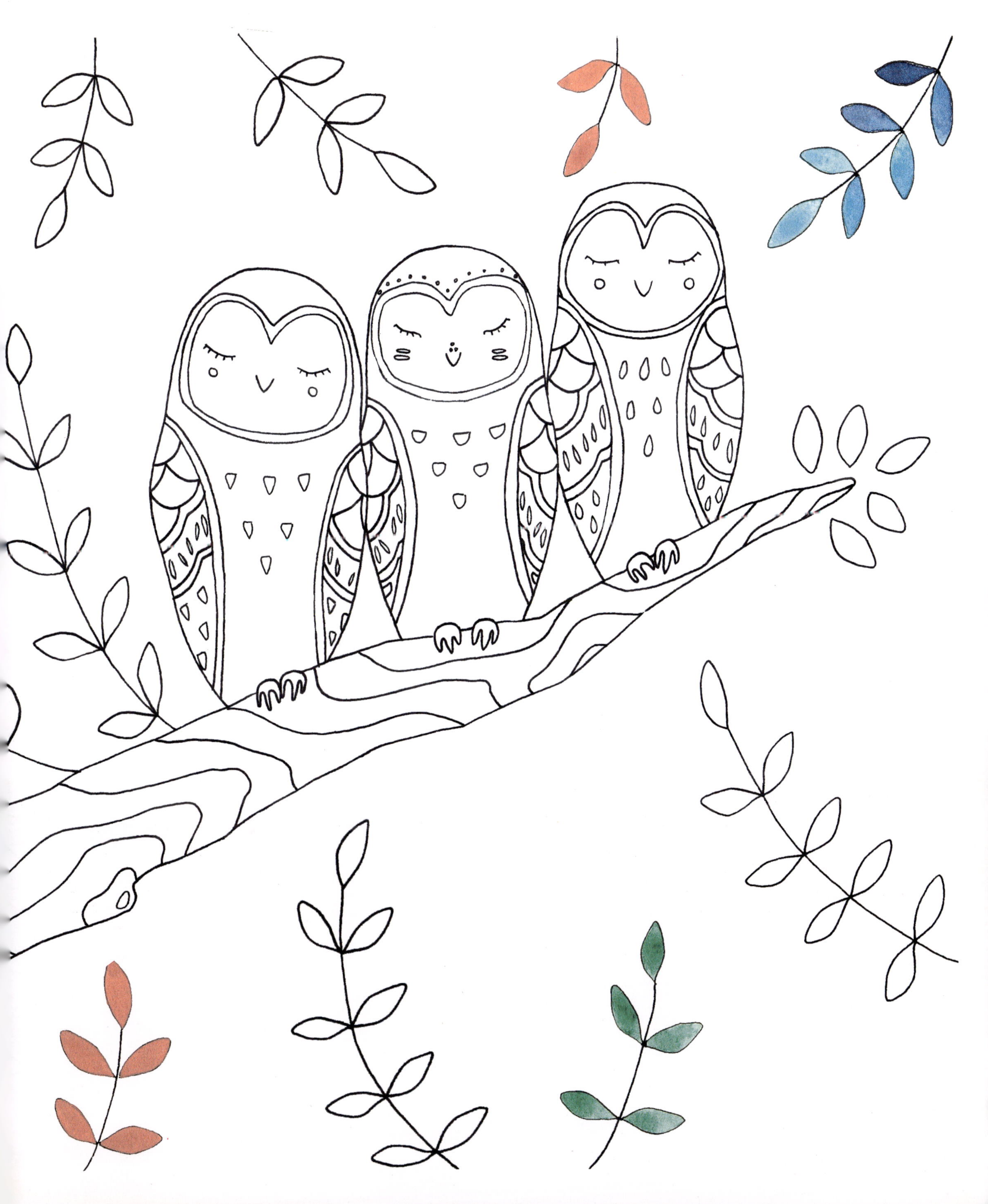

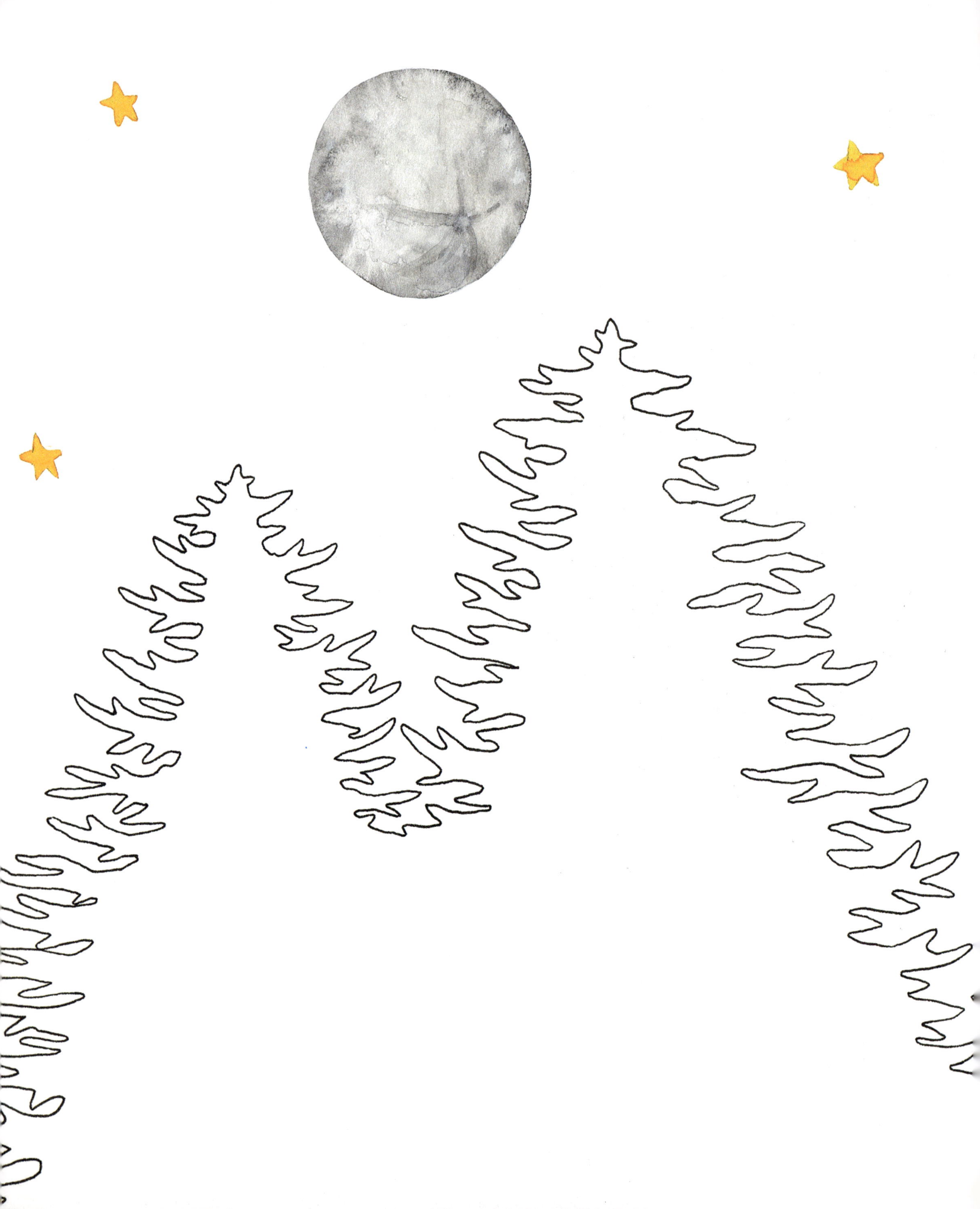

COLOR THE NIGHT SKY AND TREES. ADD STAR STICKERS
IN THE SKY AND GATHER OWL FAMILIES IN THE TREES.

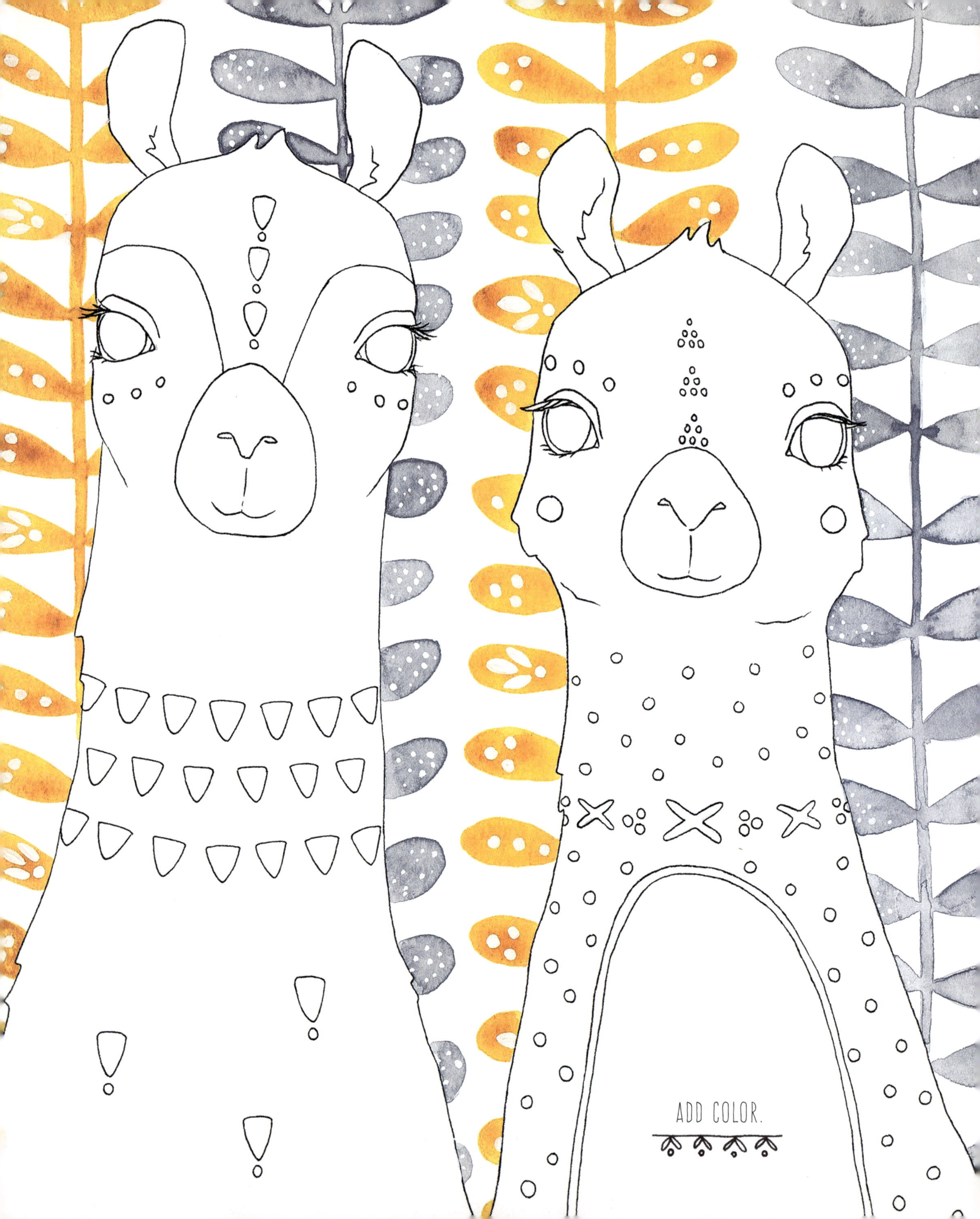
ADD COLOR.

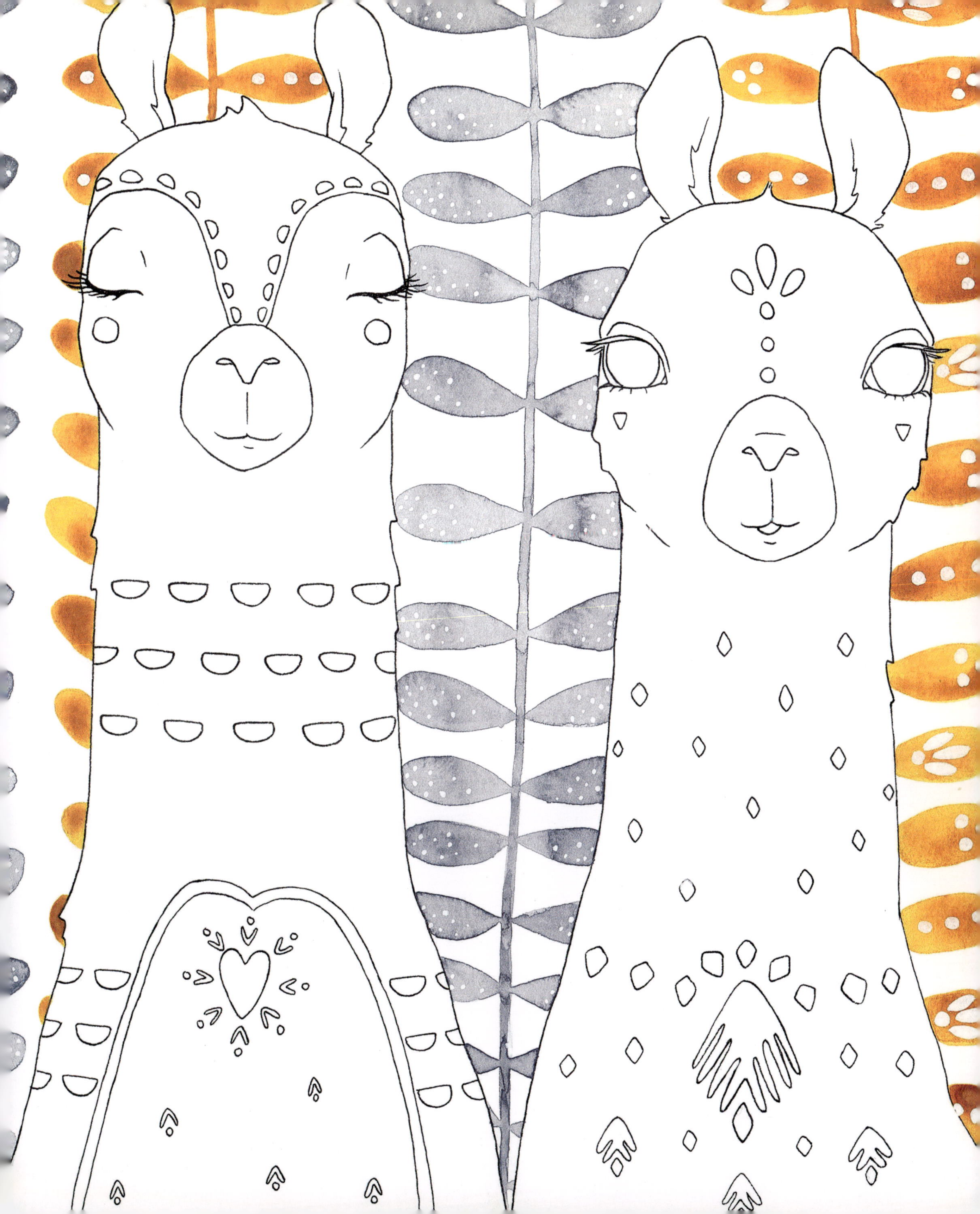

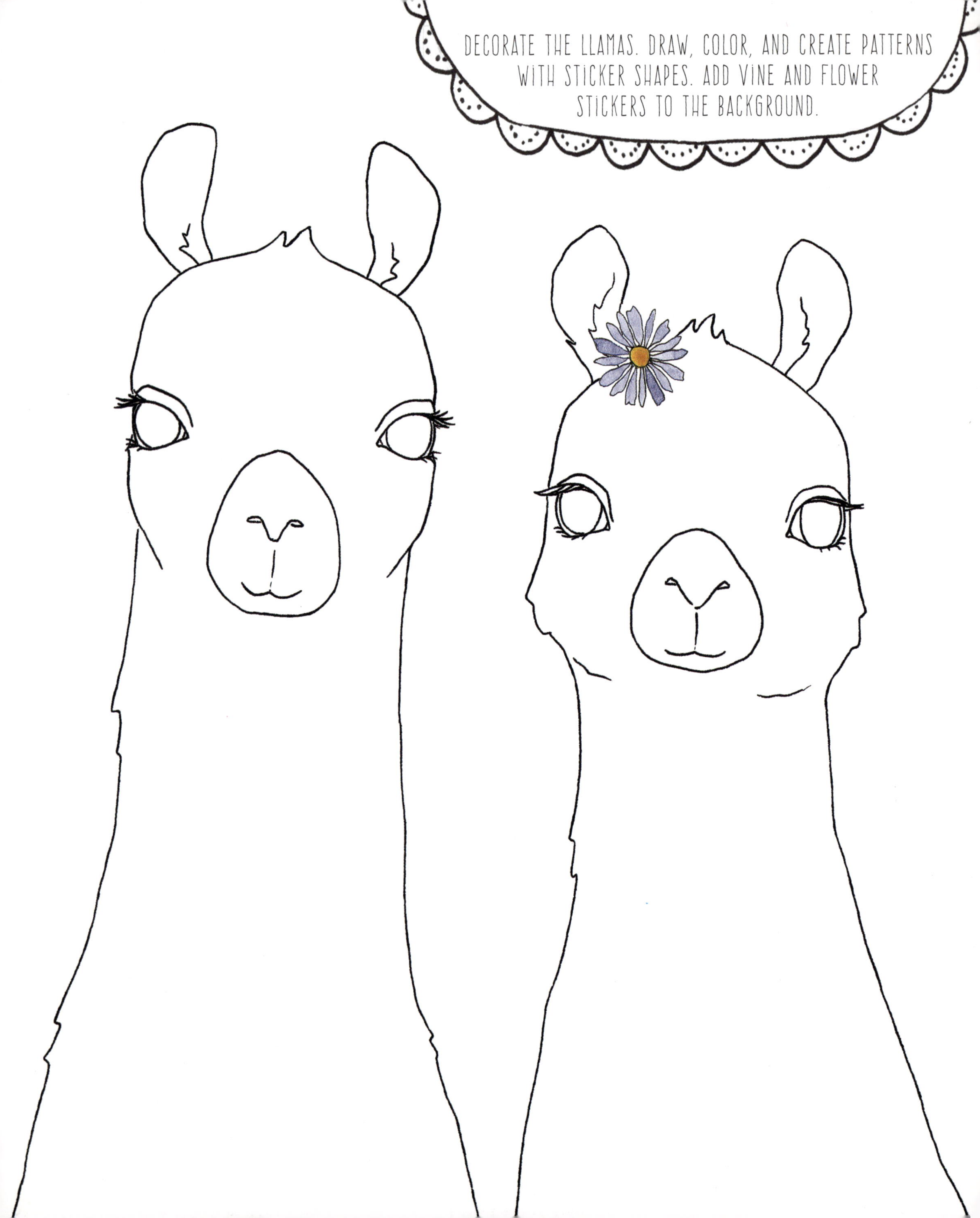

DECORATE THE LLAMAS. DRAW, COLOR, AND CREATE PATTERNS WITH STICKER SHAPES. ADD VINE AND FLOWER STICKERS TO THE BACKGROUND.

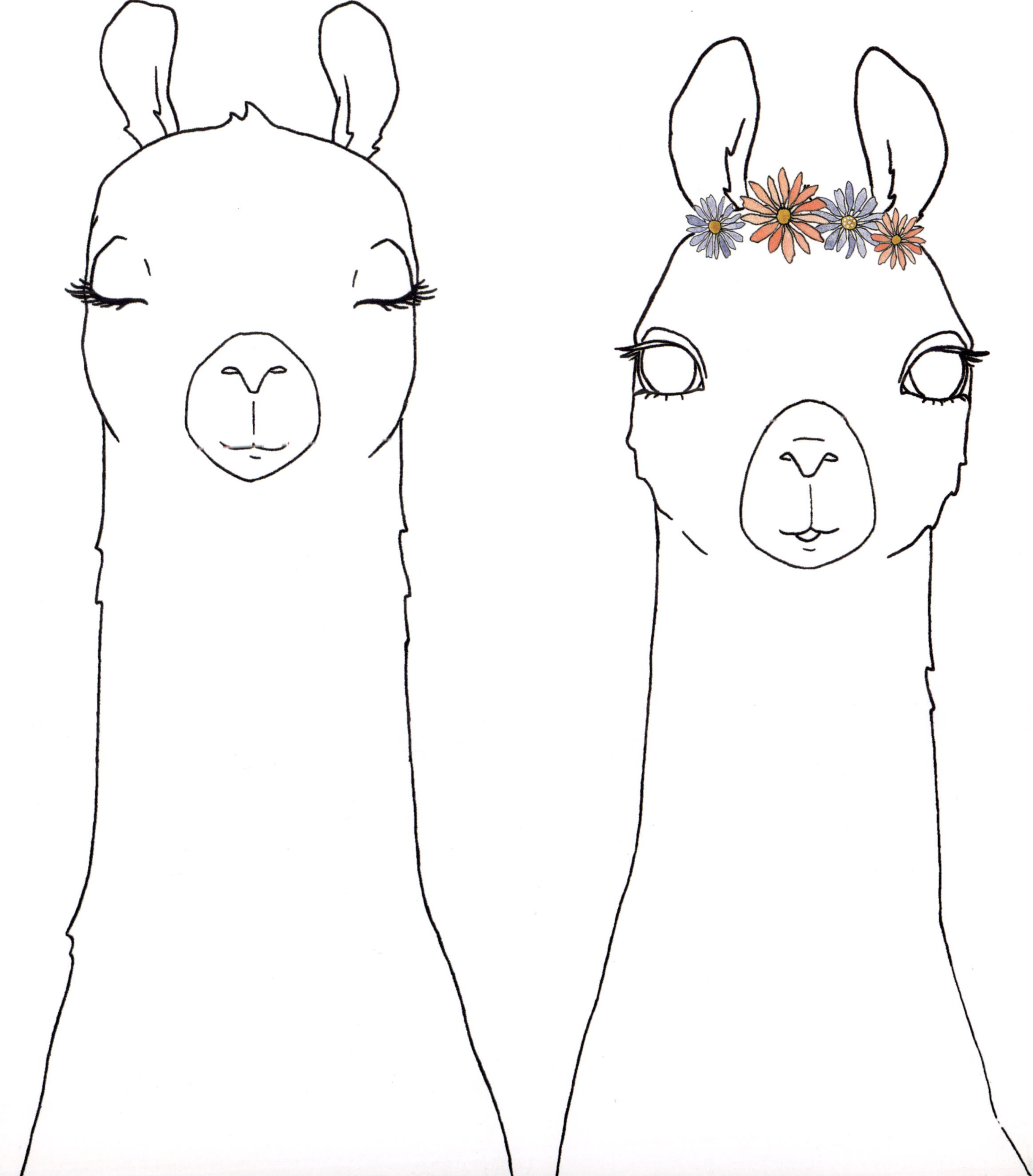

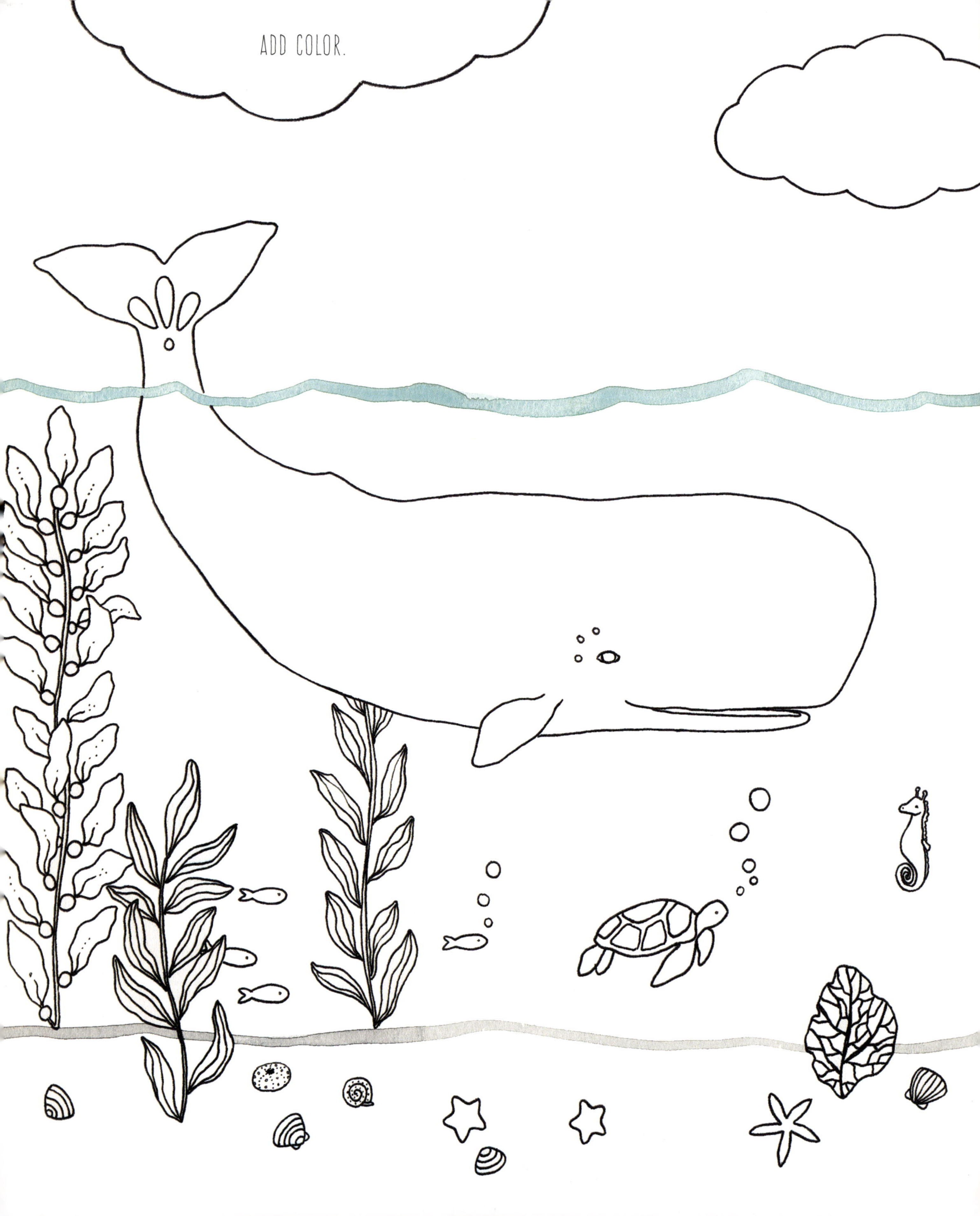
ADD COLOR.

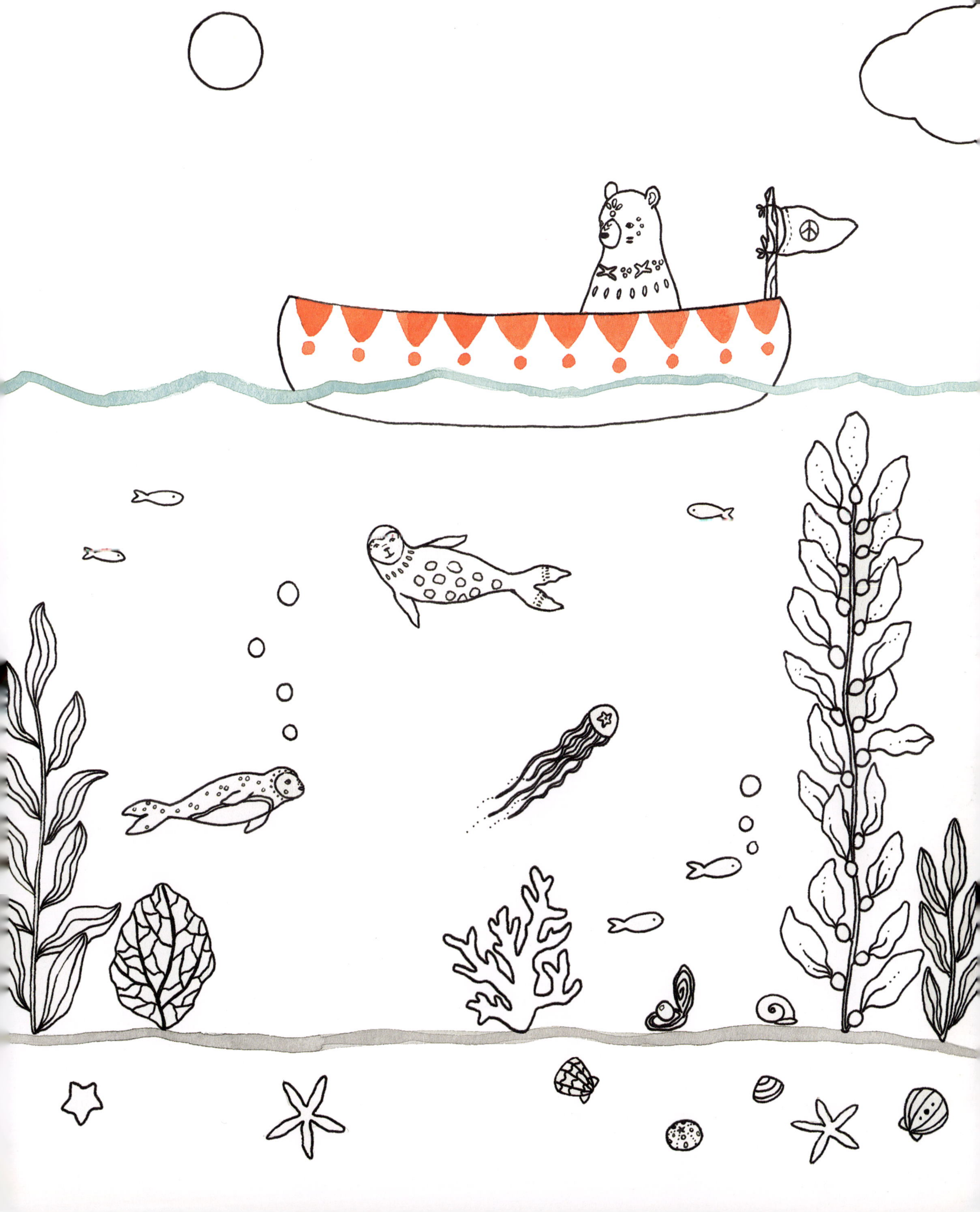

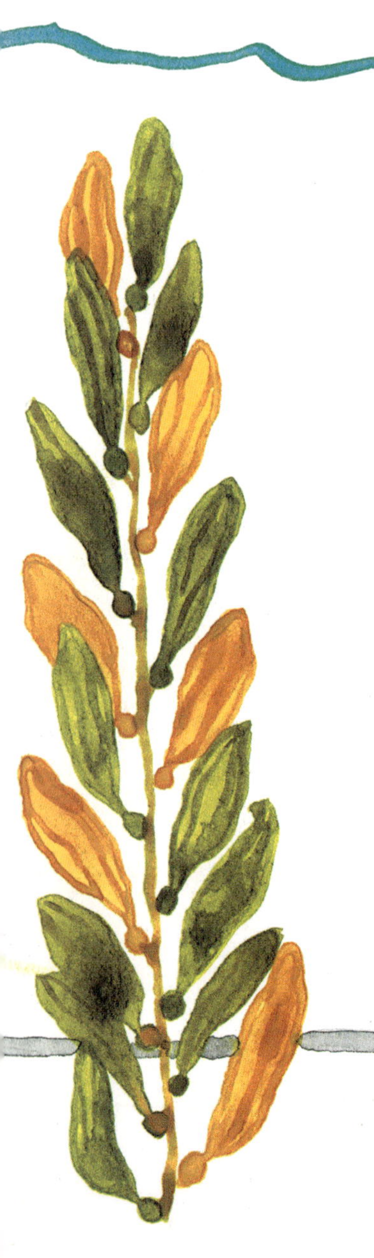

DRAW, COLOR, AND STICKER THE MYSTICAL SEA.
WHO LIVES BENEATH THE SURFACE?

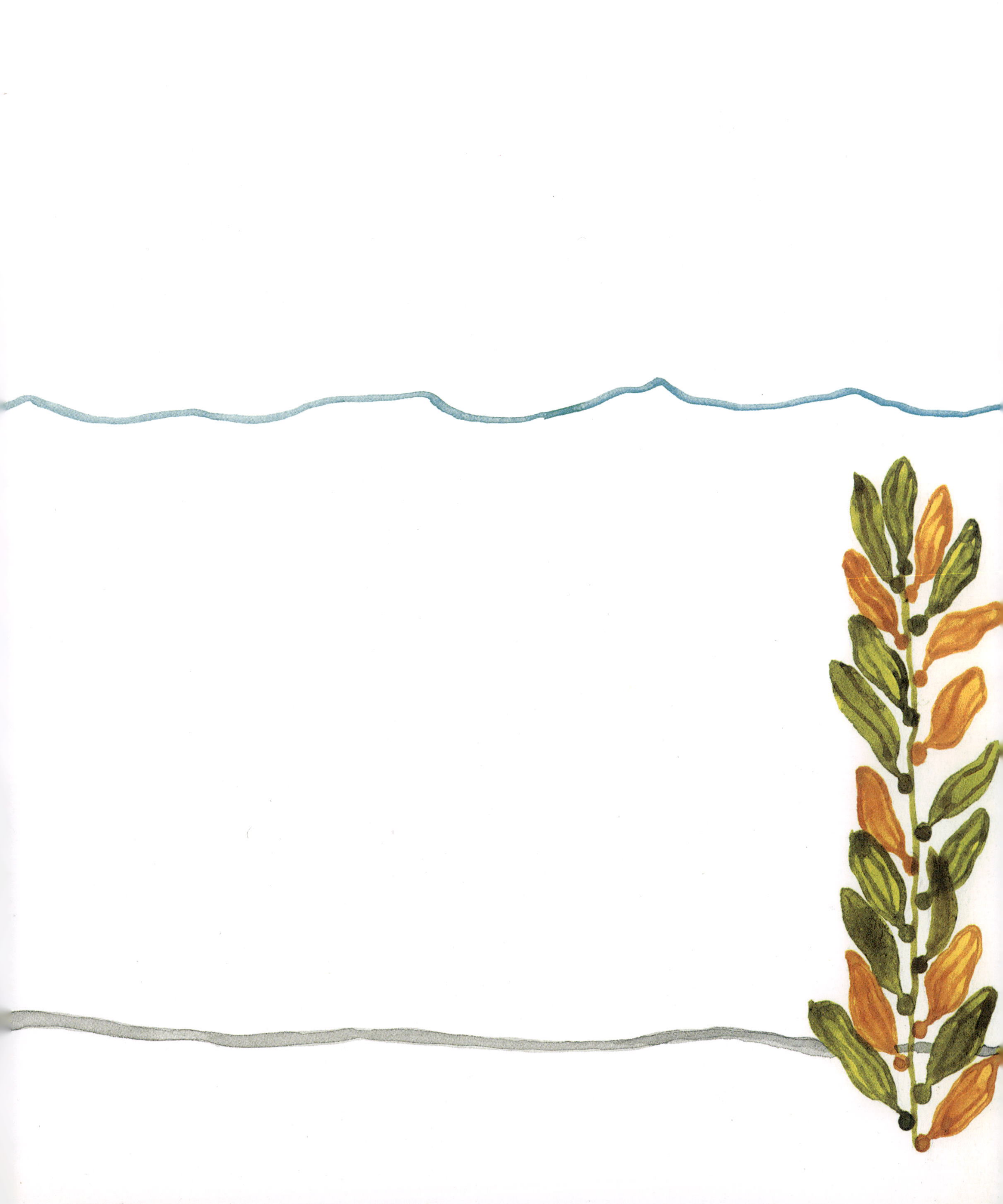

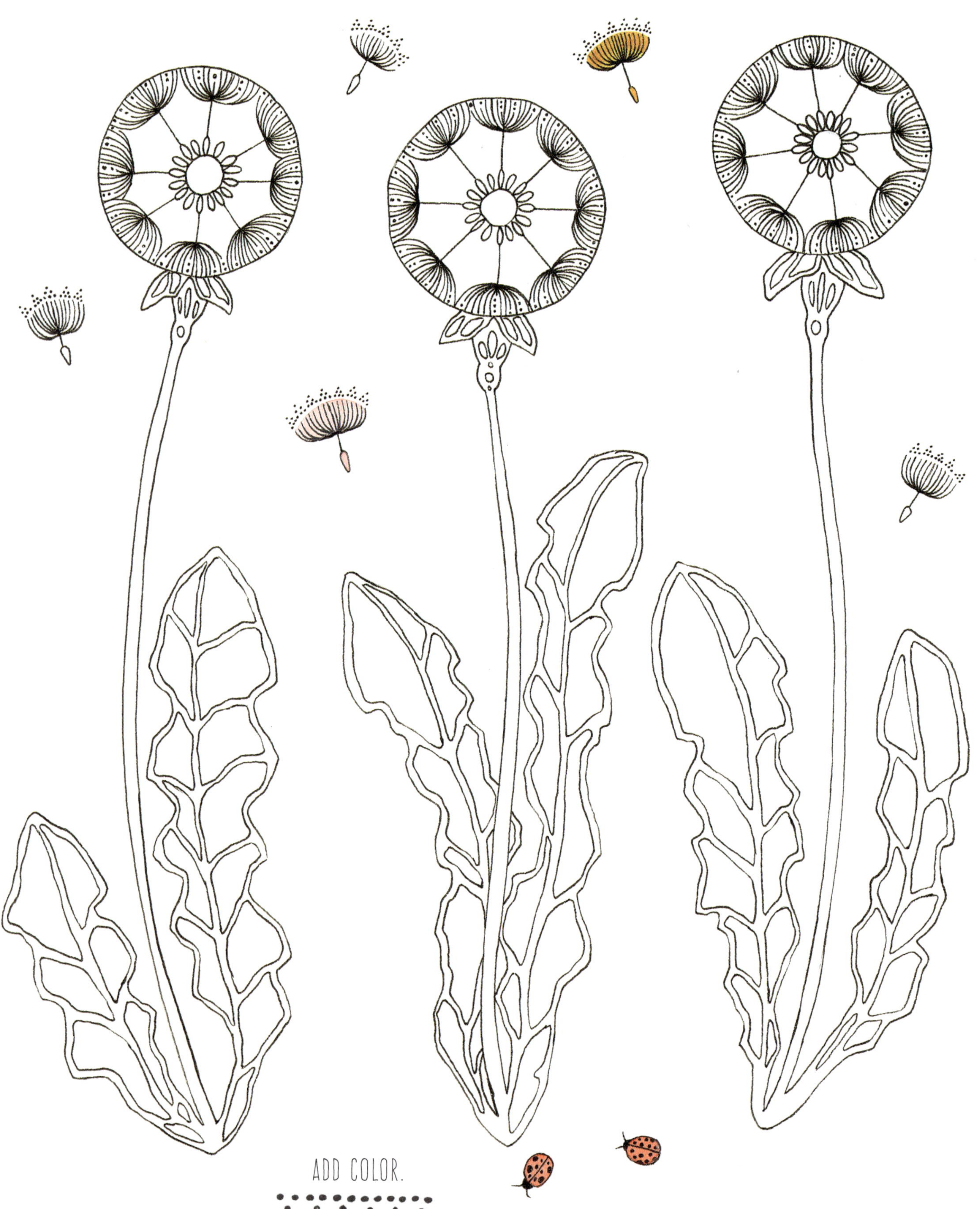
ADD COLOR.

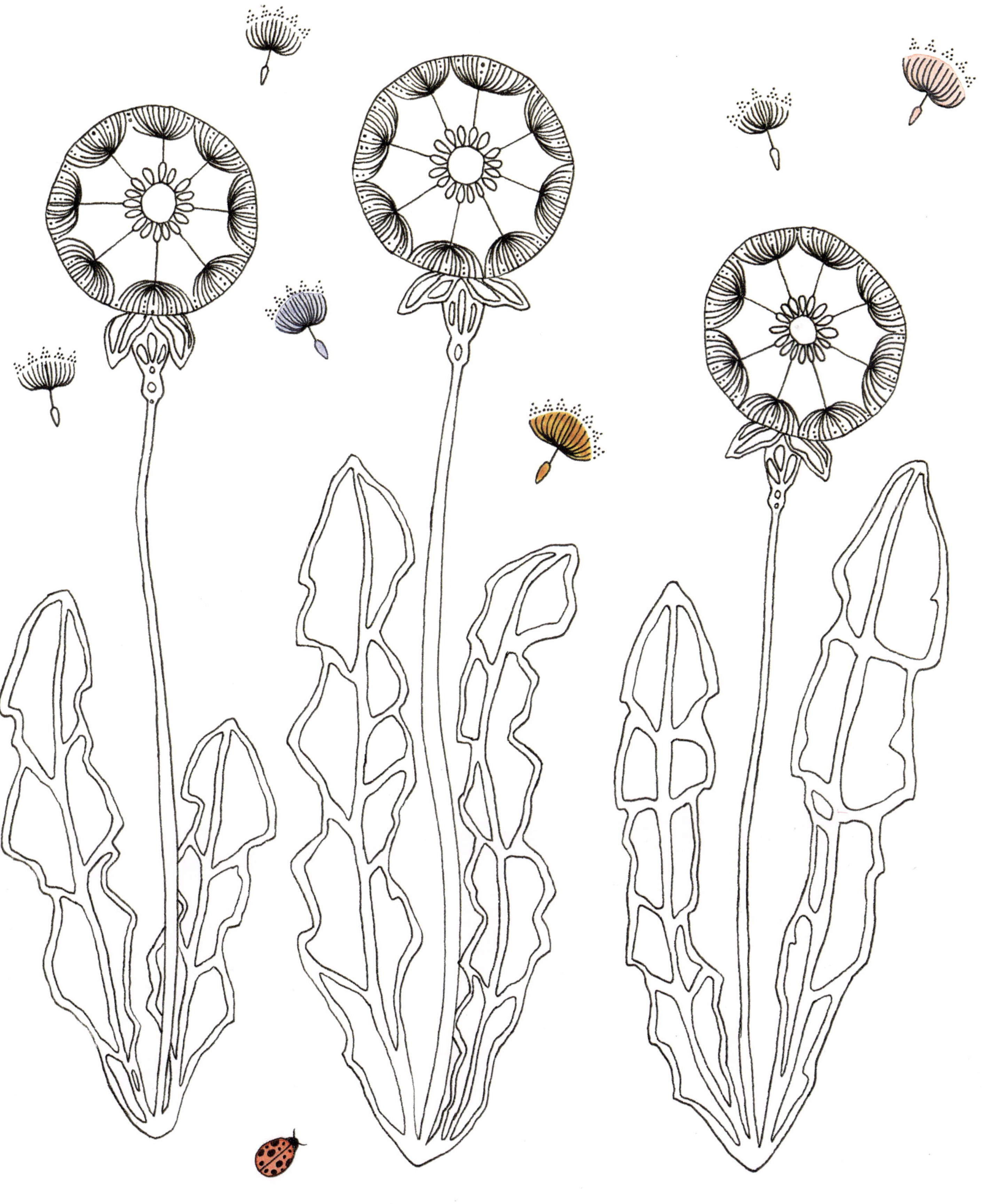

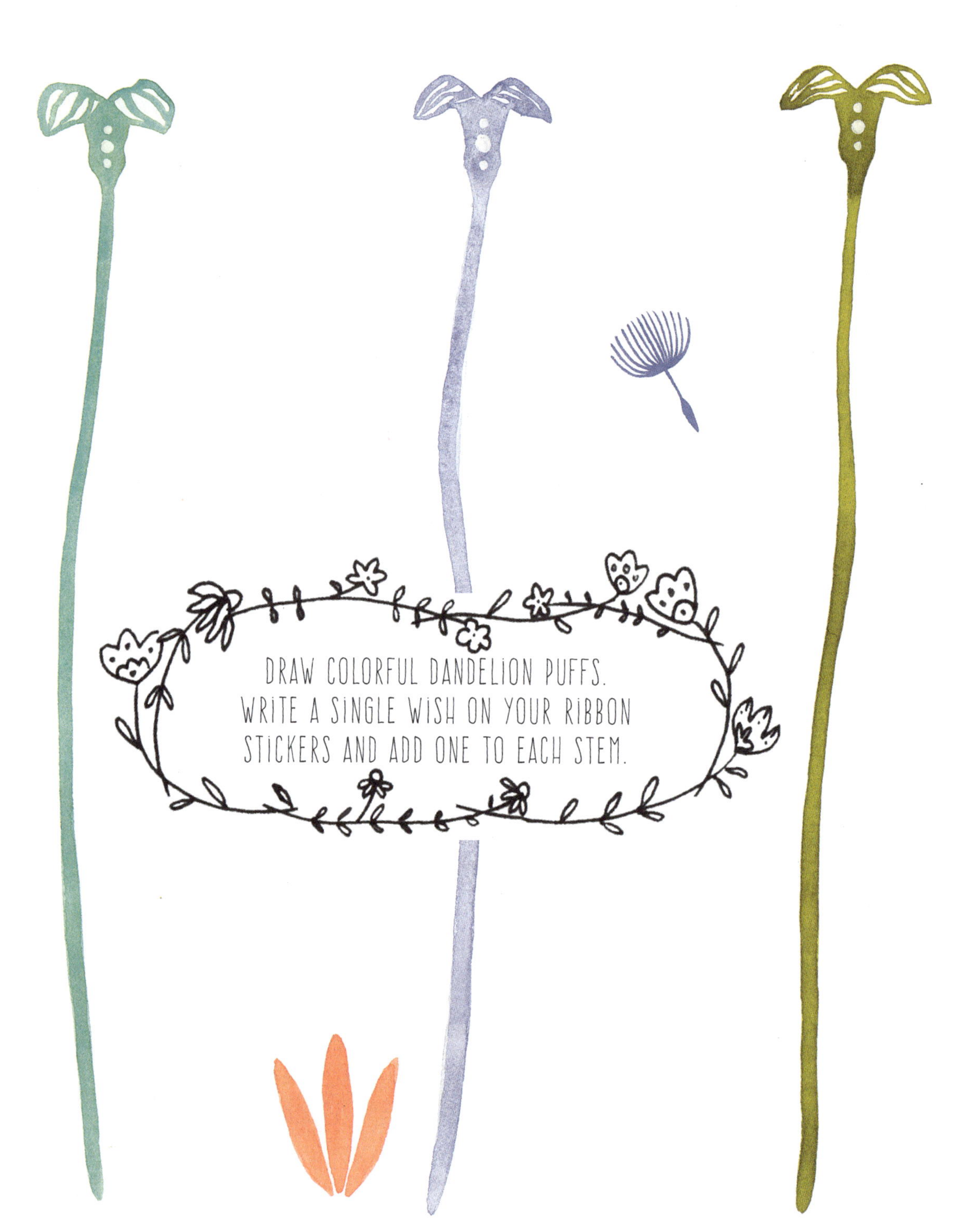

DRAW COLORFUL DANDELION PUFFS.
WRITE A SINGLE WISH ON YOUR RIBBON
STICKERS AND ADD ONE TO EACH STEM.

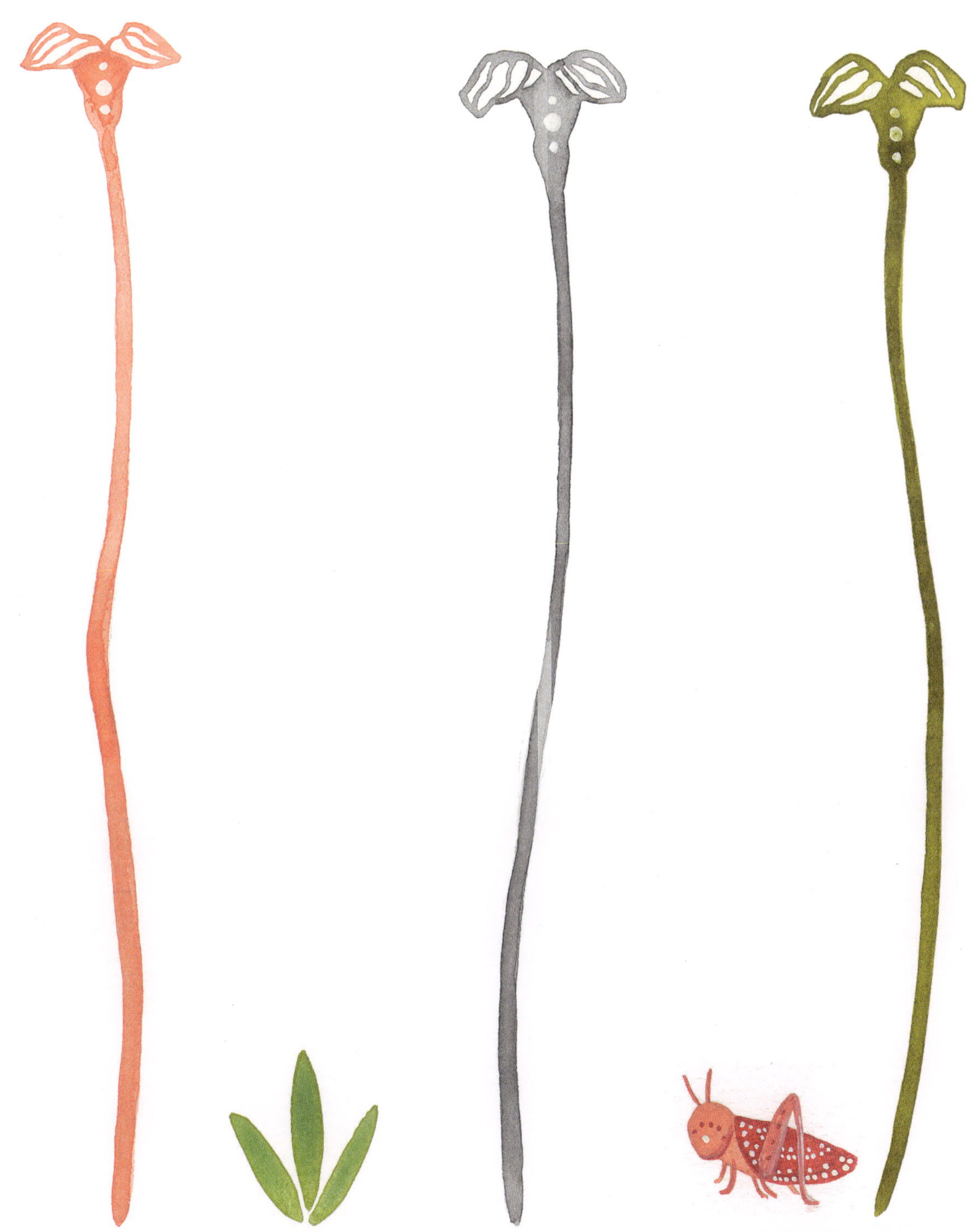

ADD COLOR.

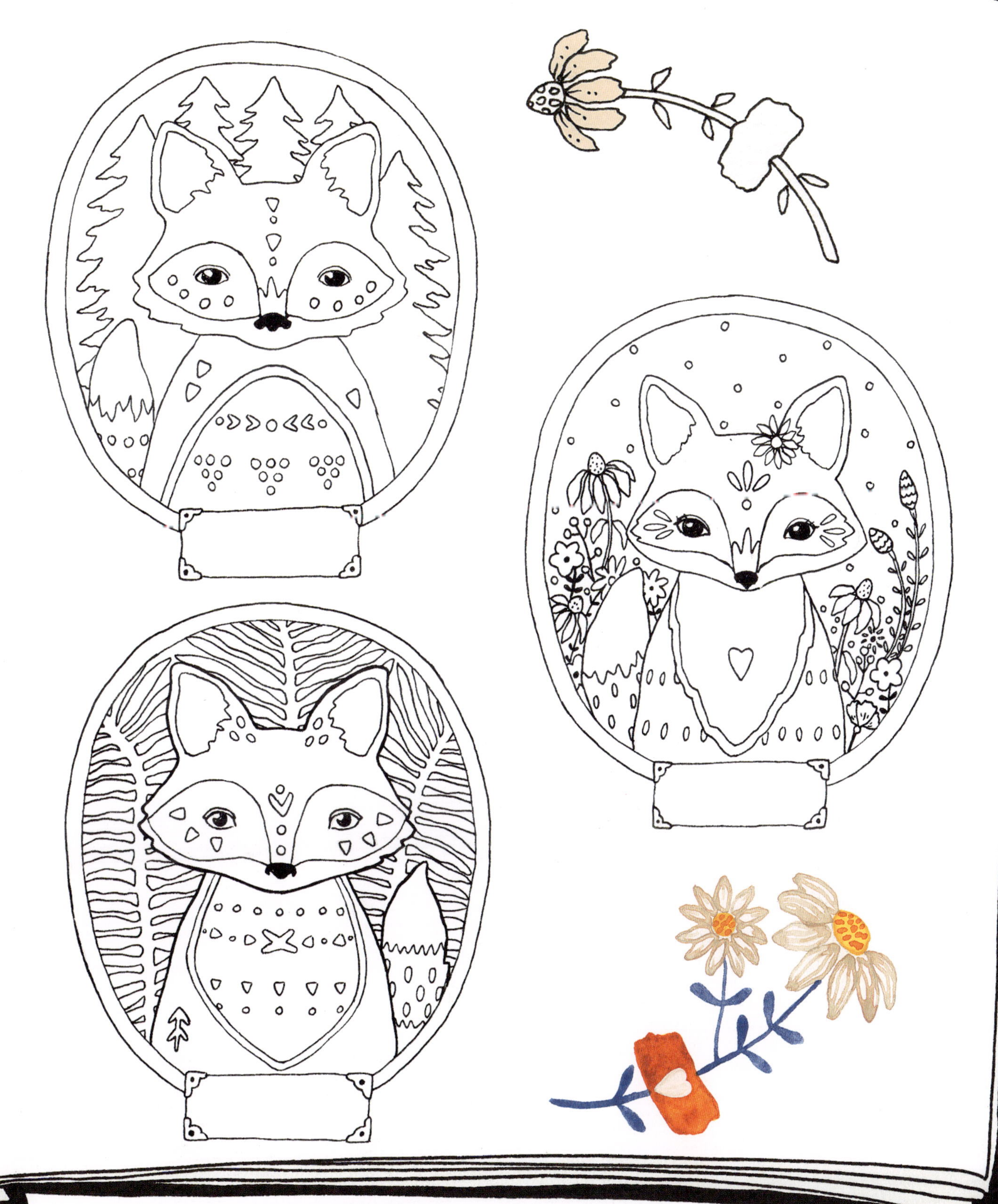

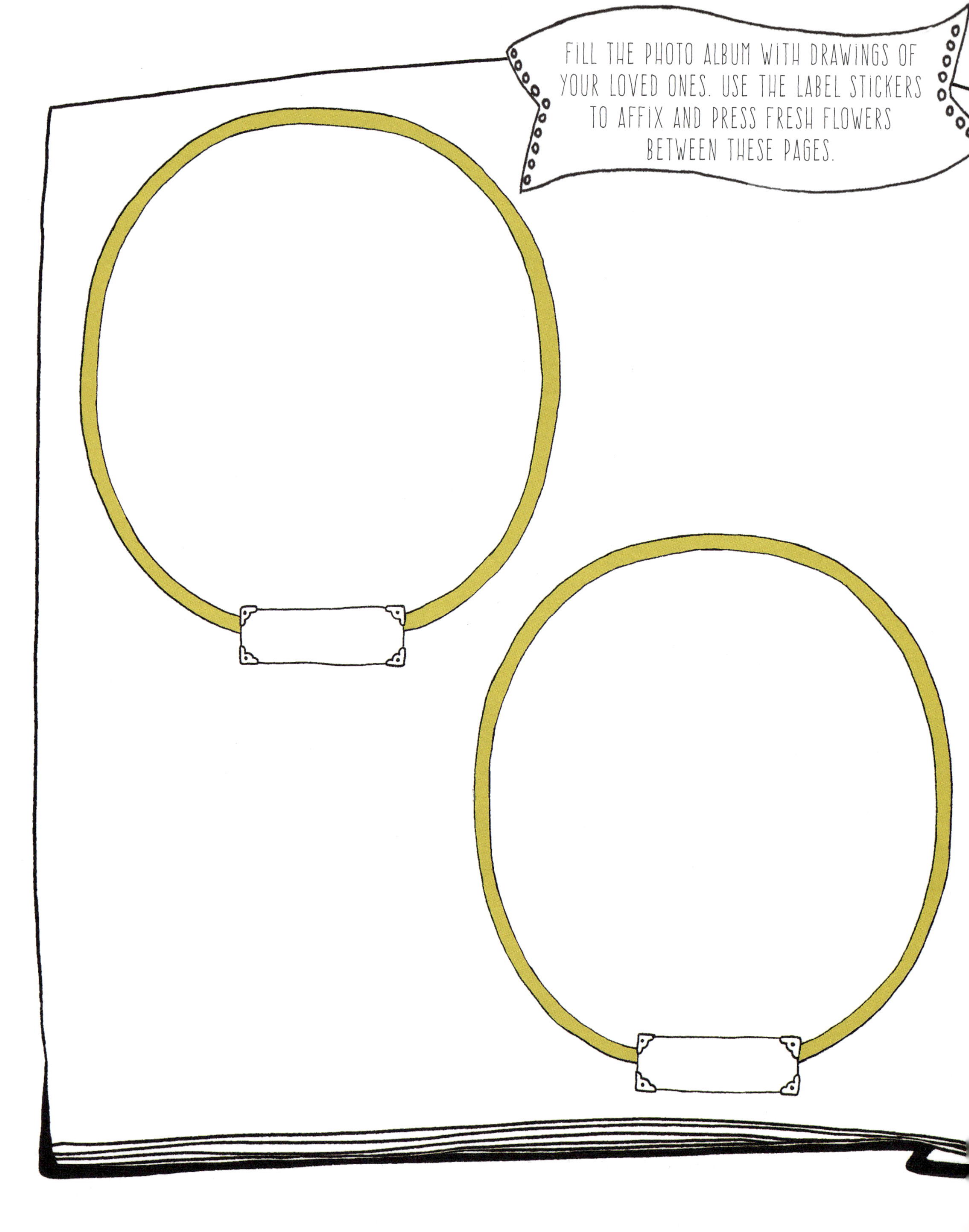
FILL THE PHOTO ALBUM WITH DRAWINGS OF
YOUR LOVED ONES. USE THE LABEL STICKERS
TO AFFIX AND PRESS FRESH FLOWERS
BETWEEN THESE PAGES.

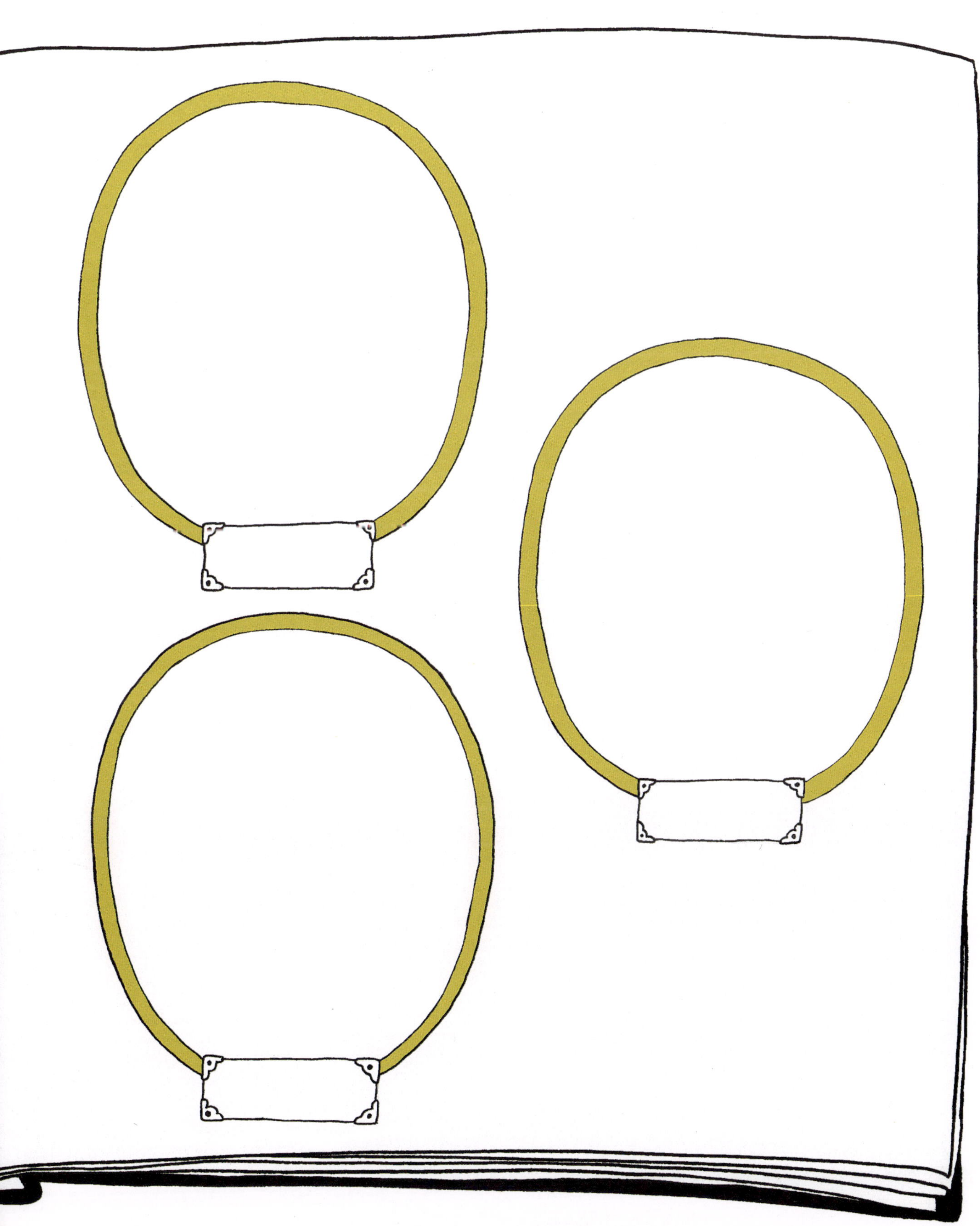

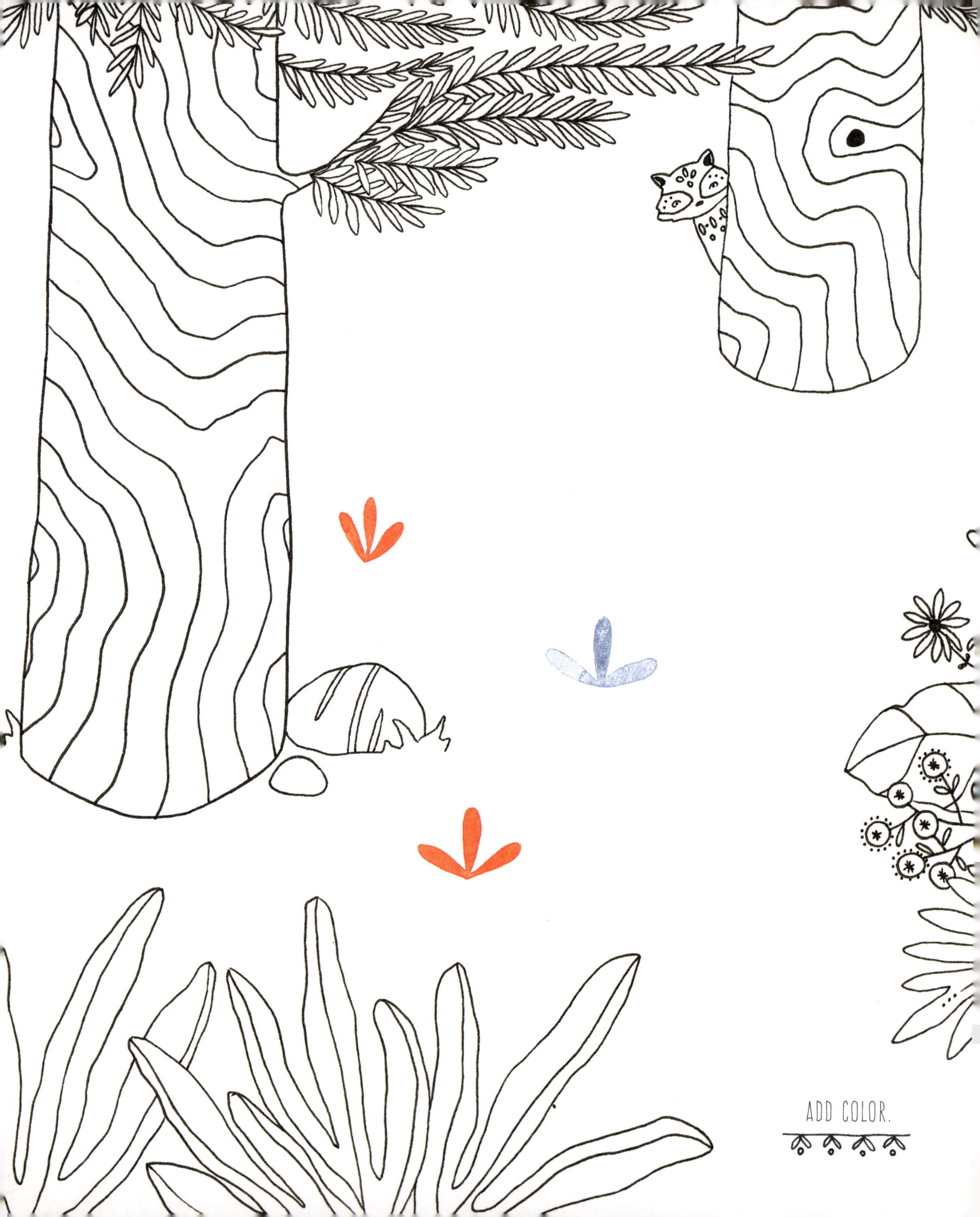
ADD COLOR.

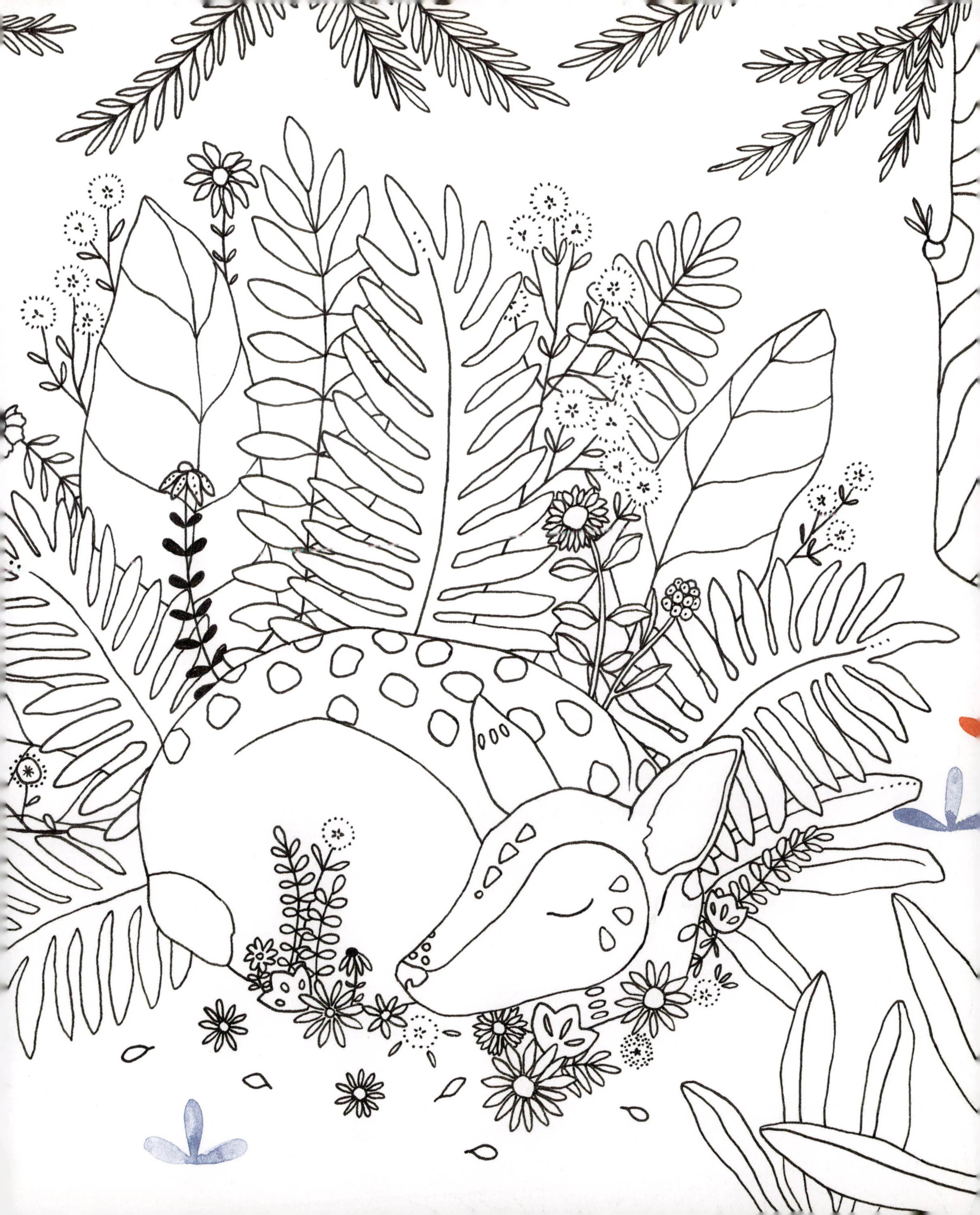

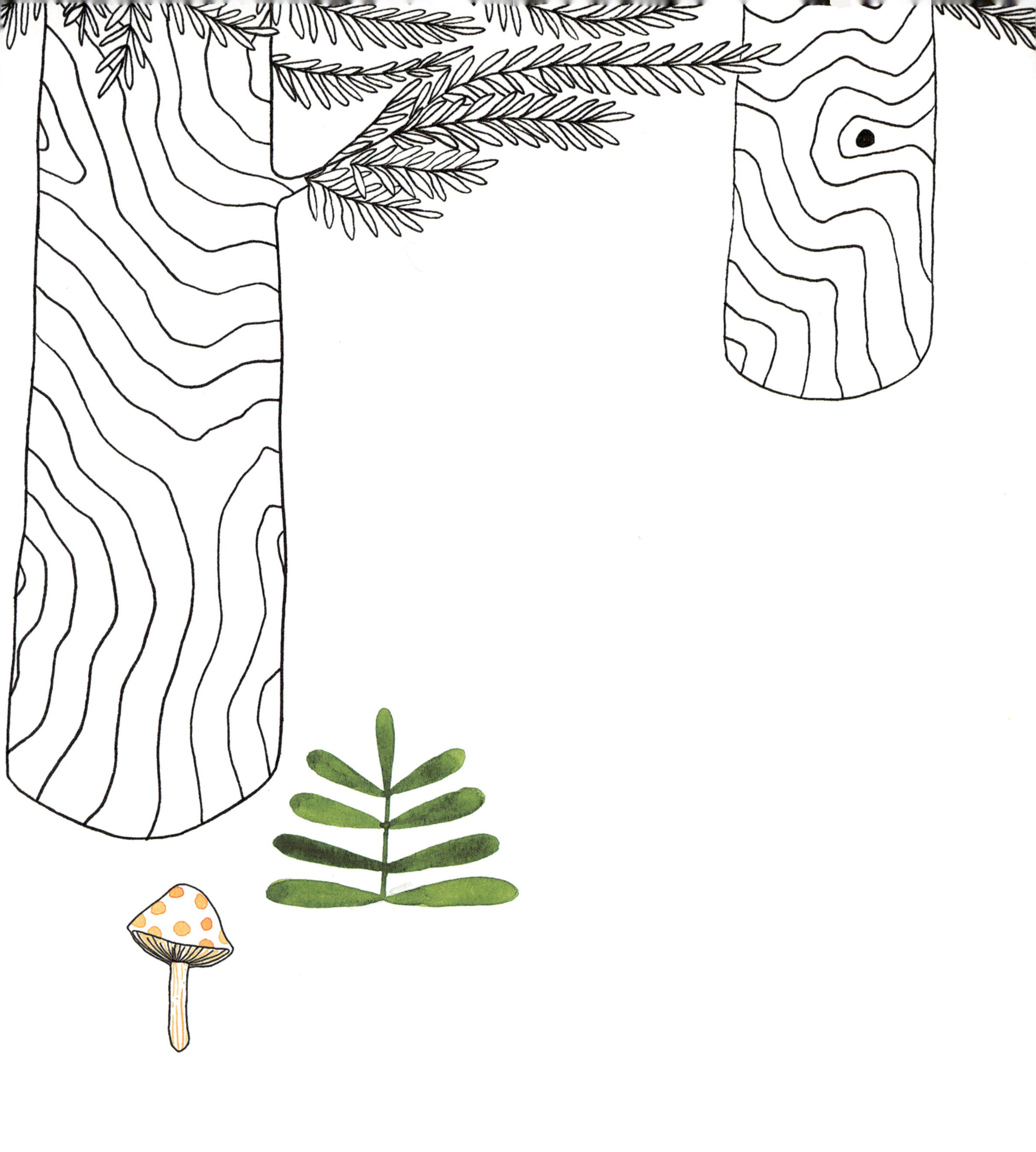

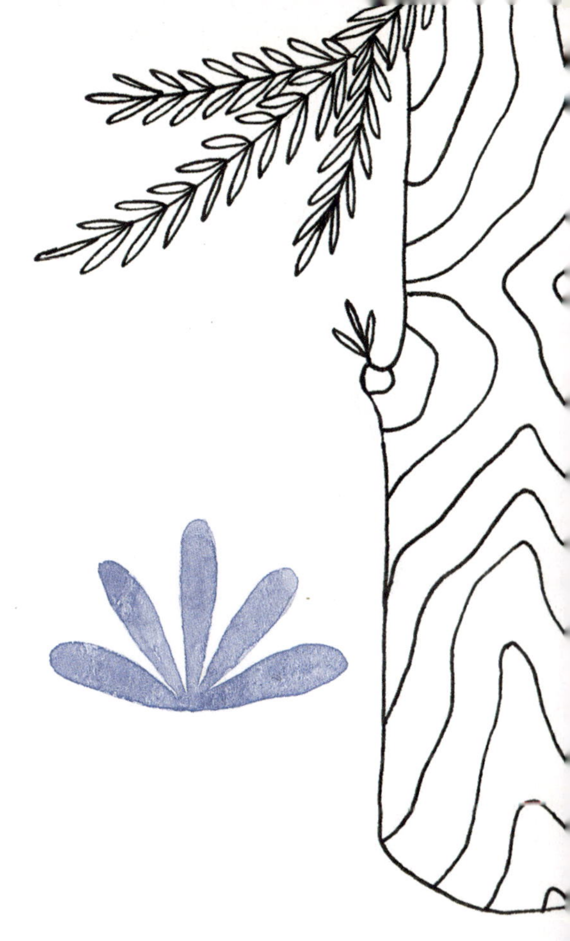

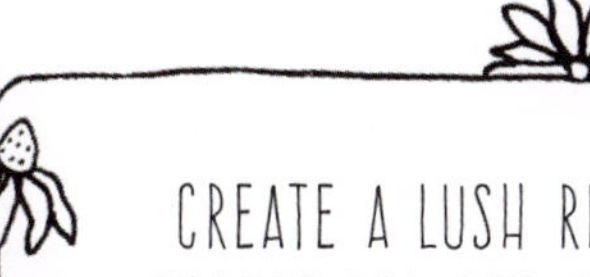
CREATE A LUSH RESTING SPACE IN THE
FOREST FOR THE SLEEPY FAWN STICKER.

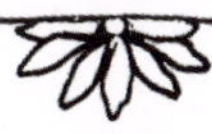

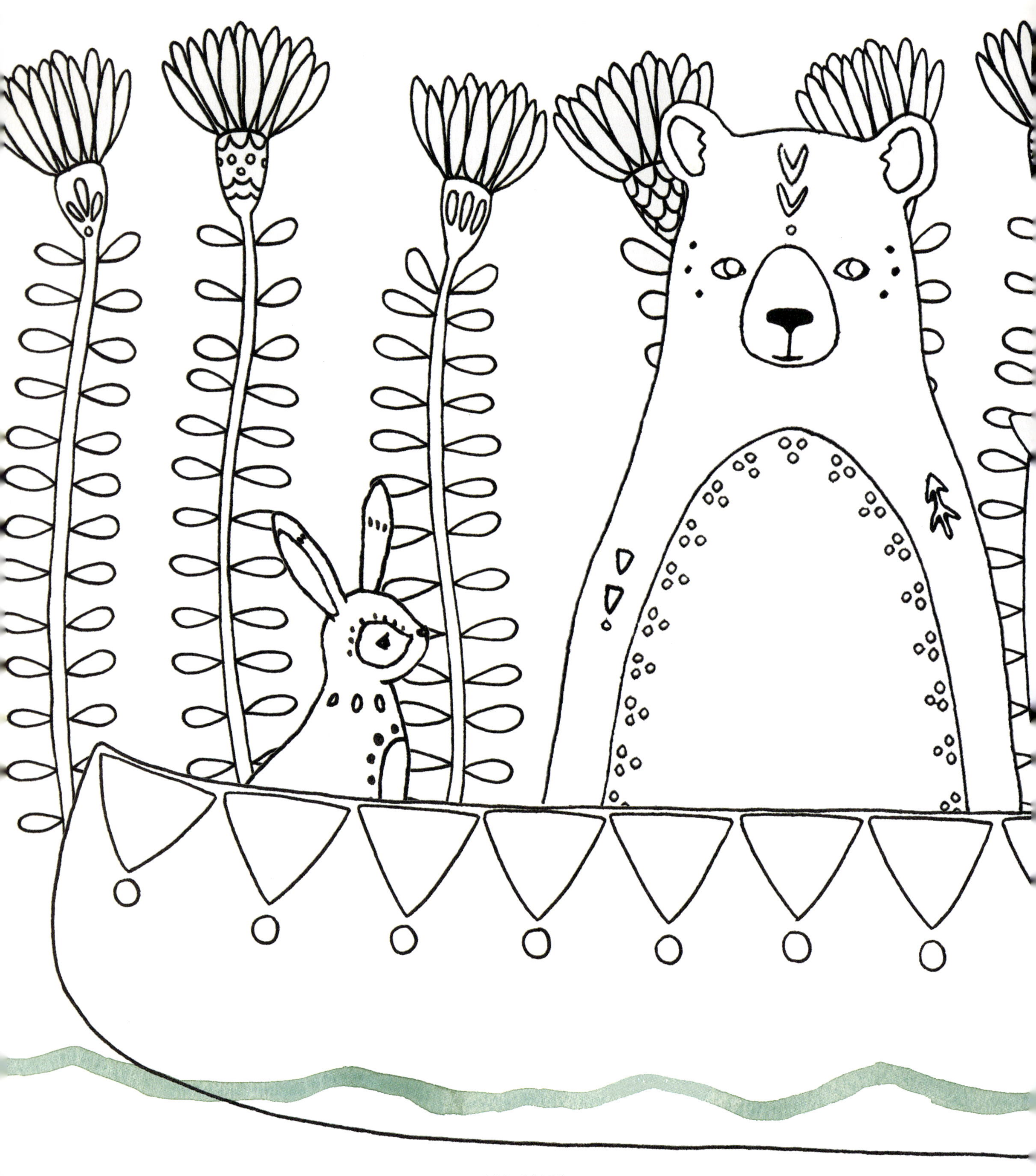

ADD COLOR.

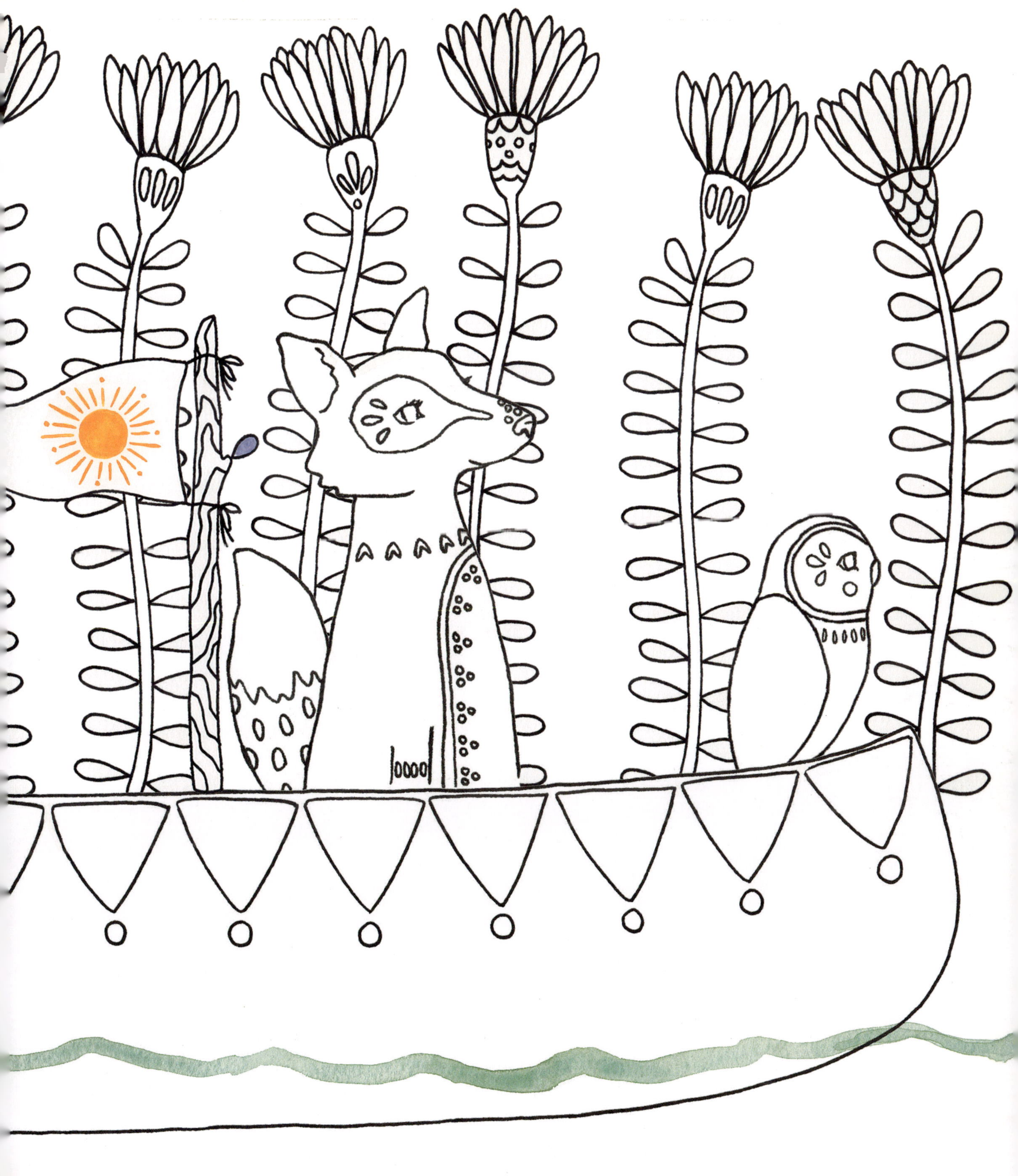

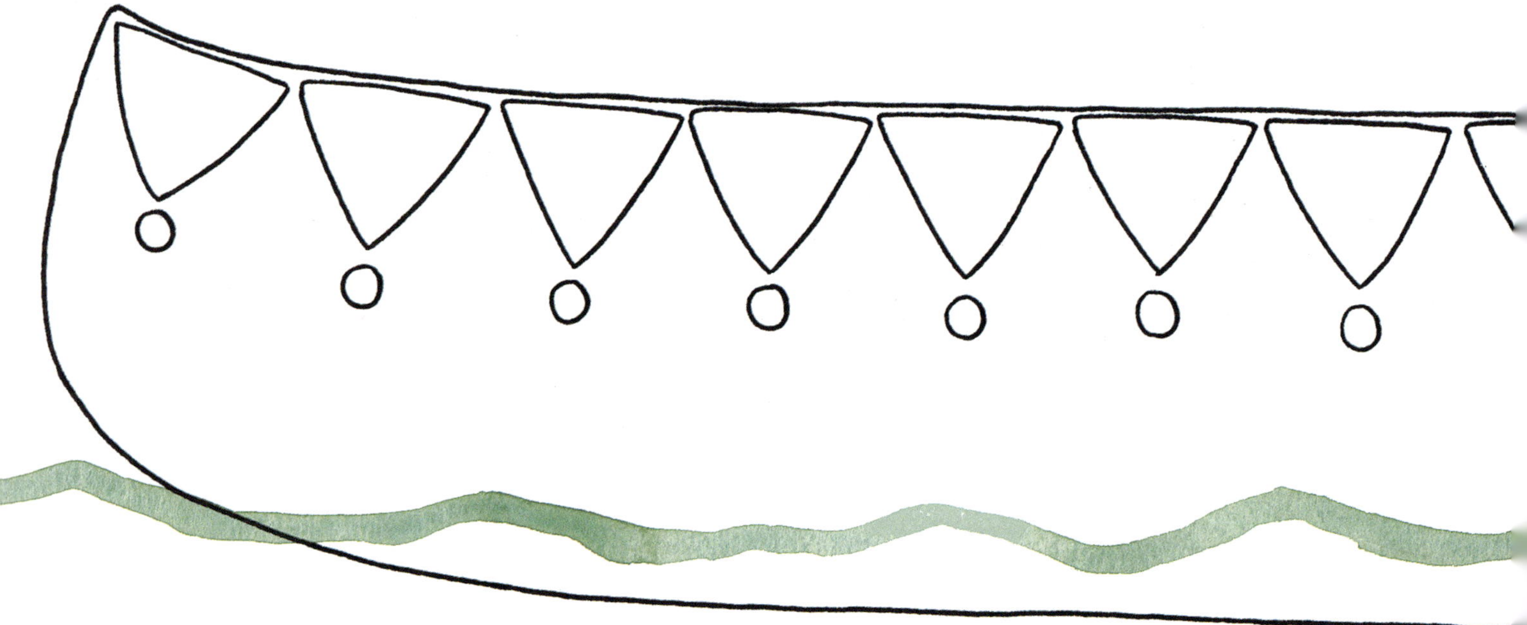

FILL THE CANOE WITH WILD ONES, GREAT AND SMALL.
ADD PATTERNS TO THE CANOE AND CREATE THE AREA THEY`RE EXPLORING.

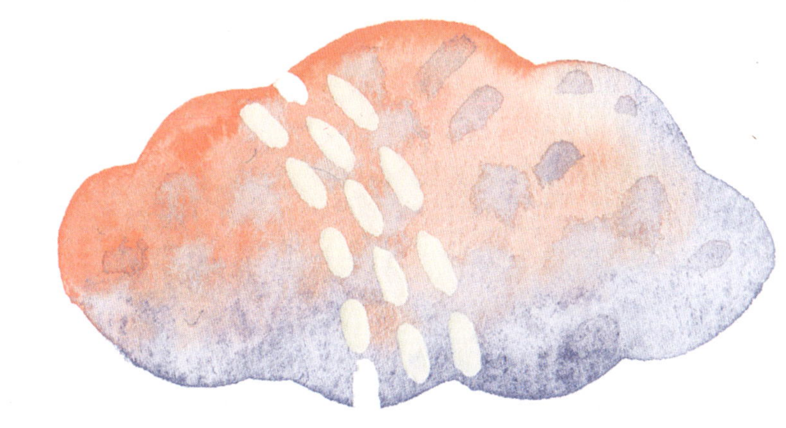
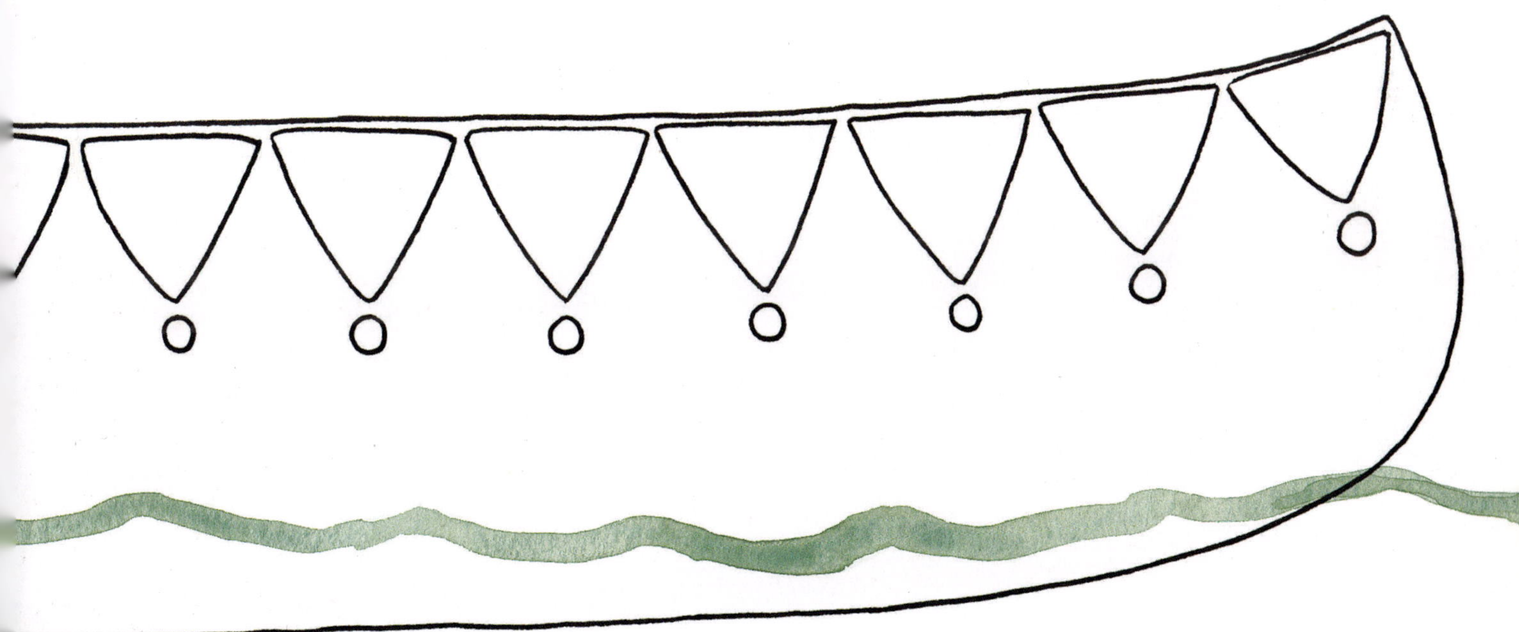

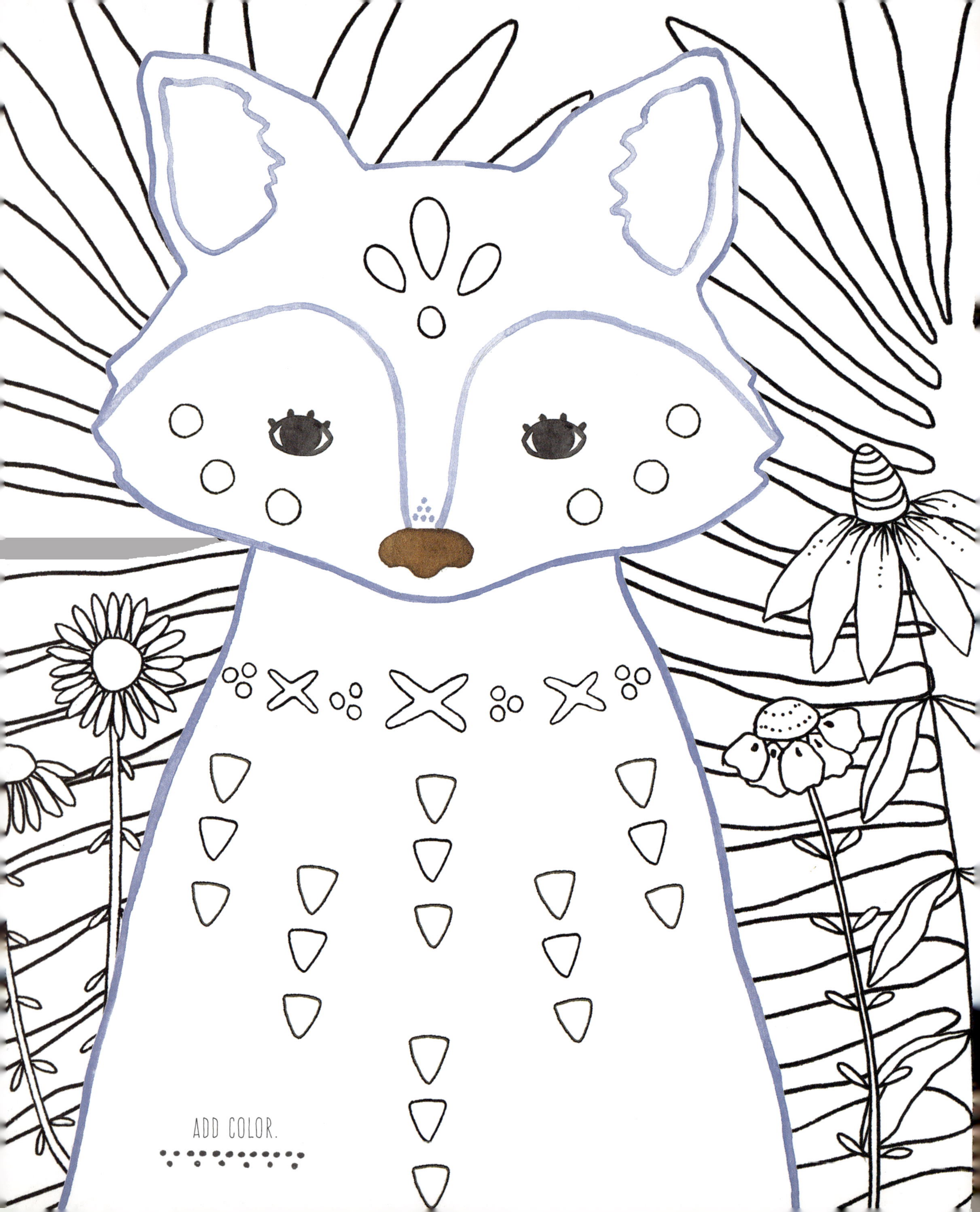
ADD COLOR.

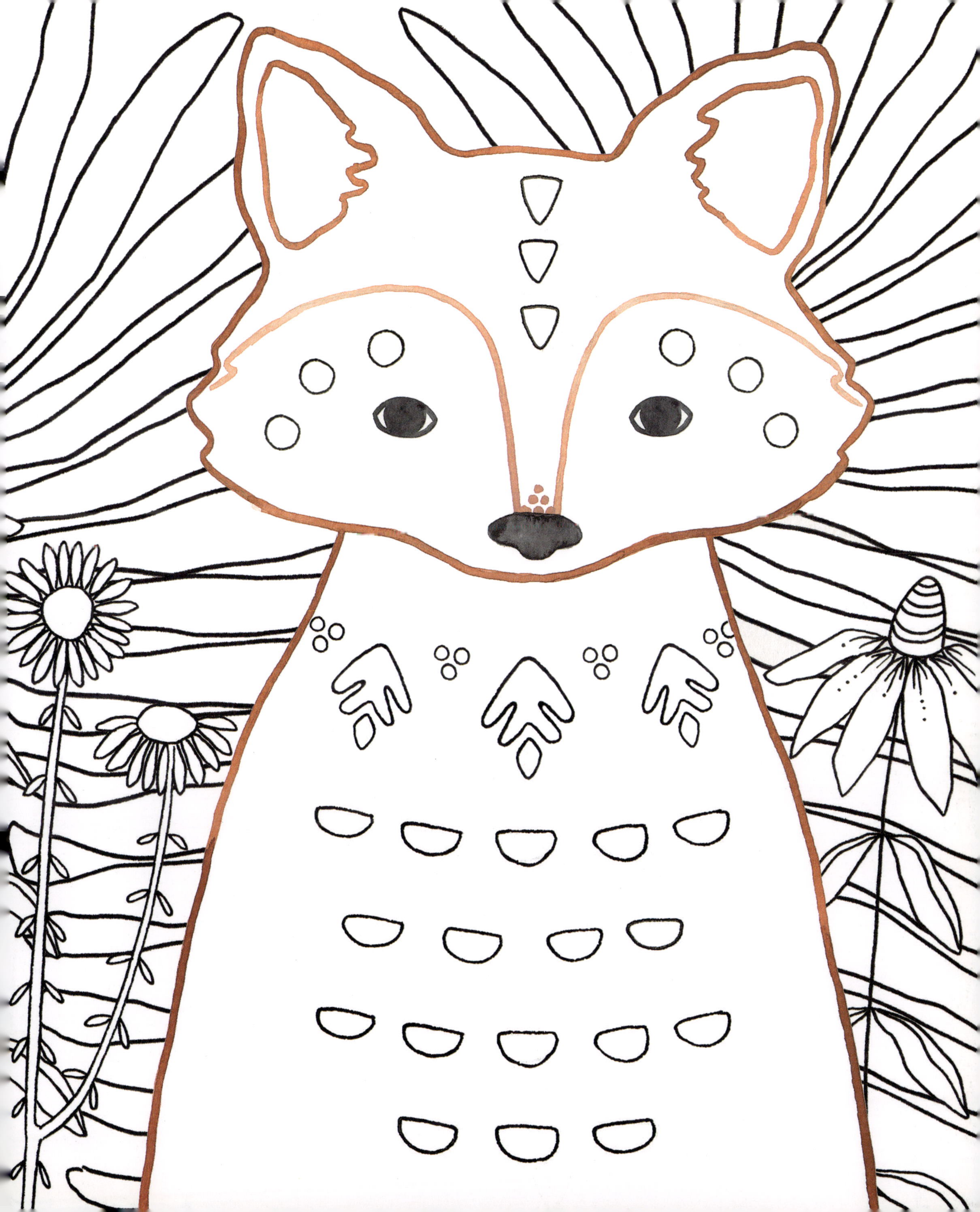

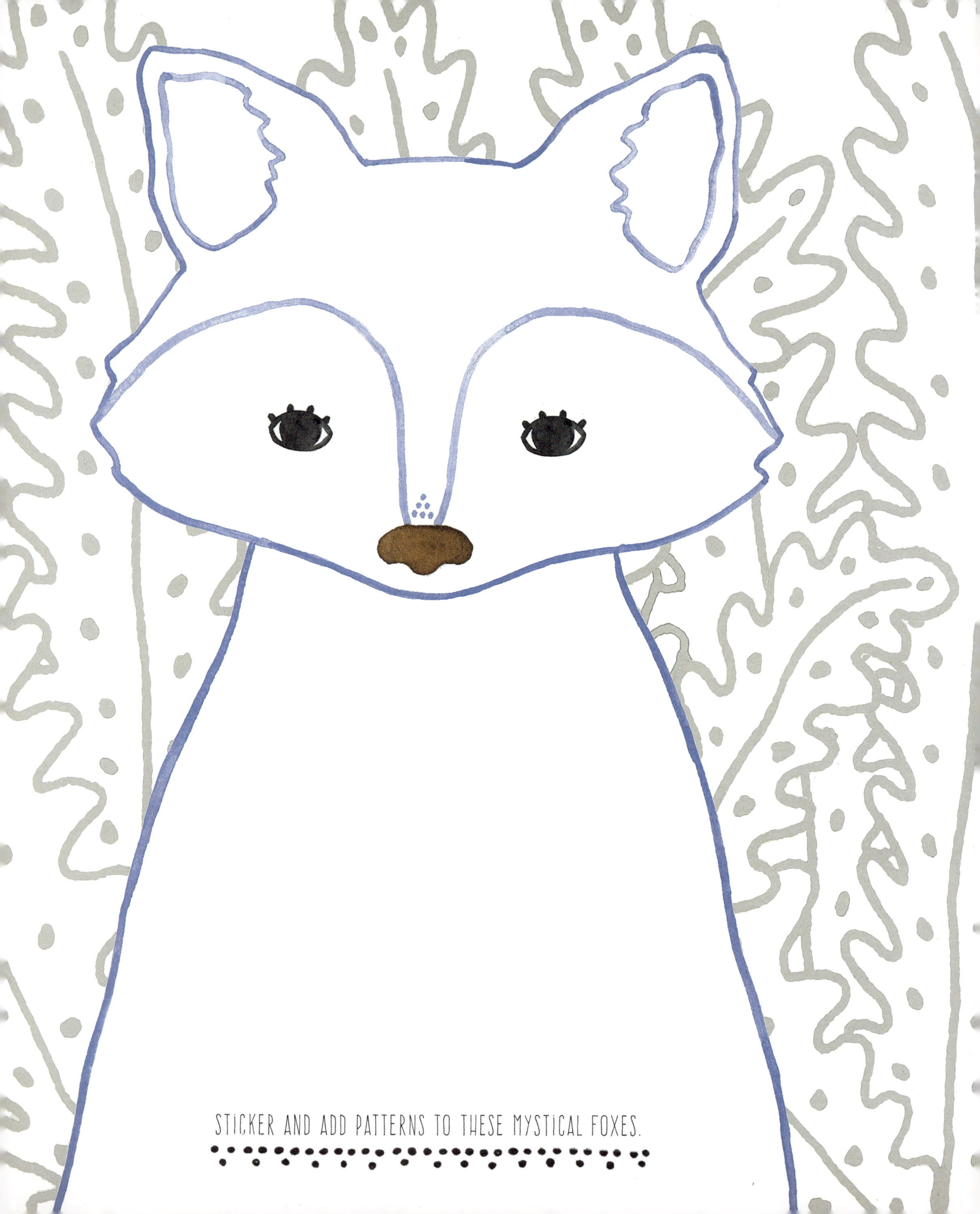

STiCKER AND ADD PATTERNS TO THESE MYSTICAL FOXES.

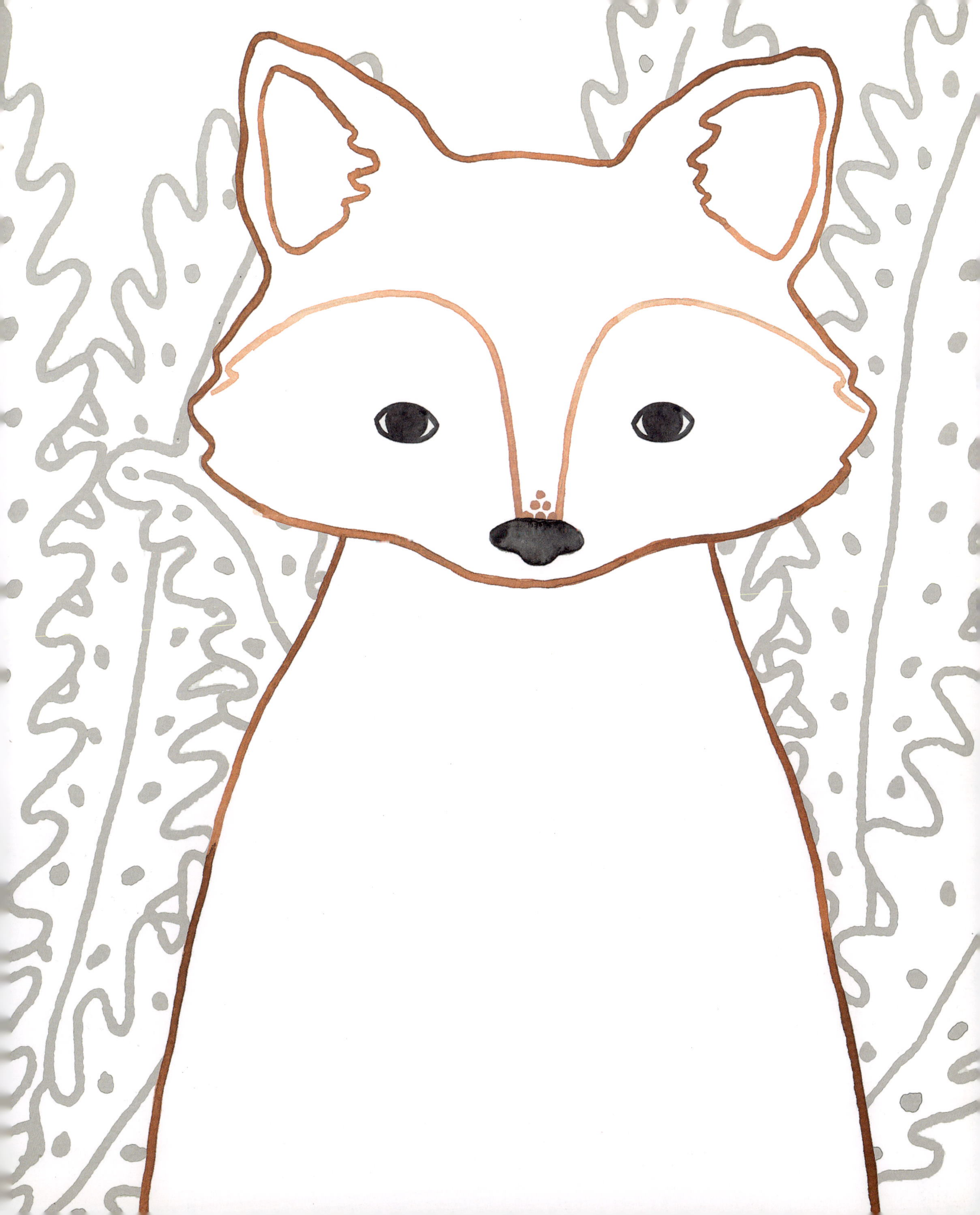

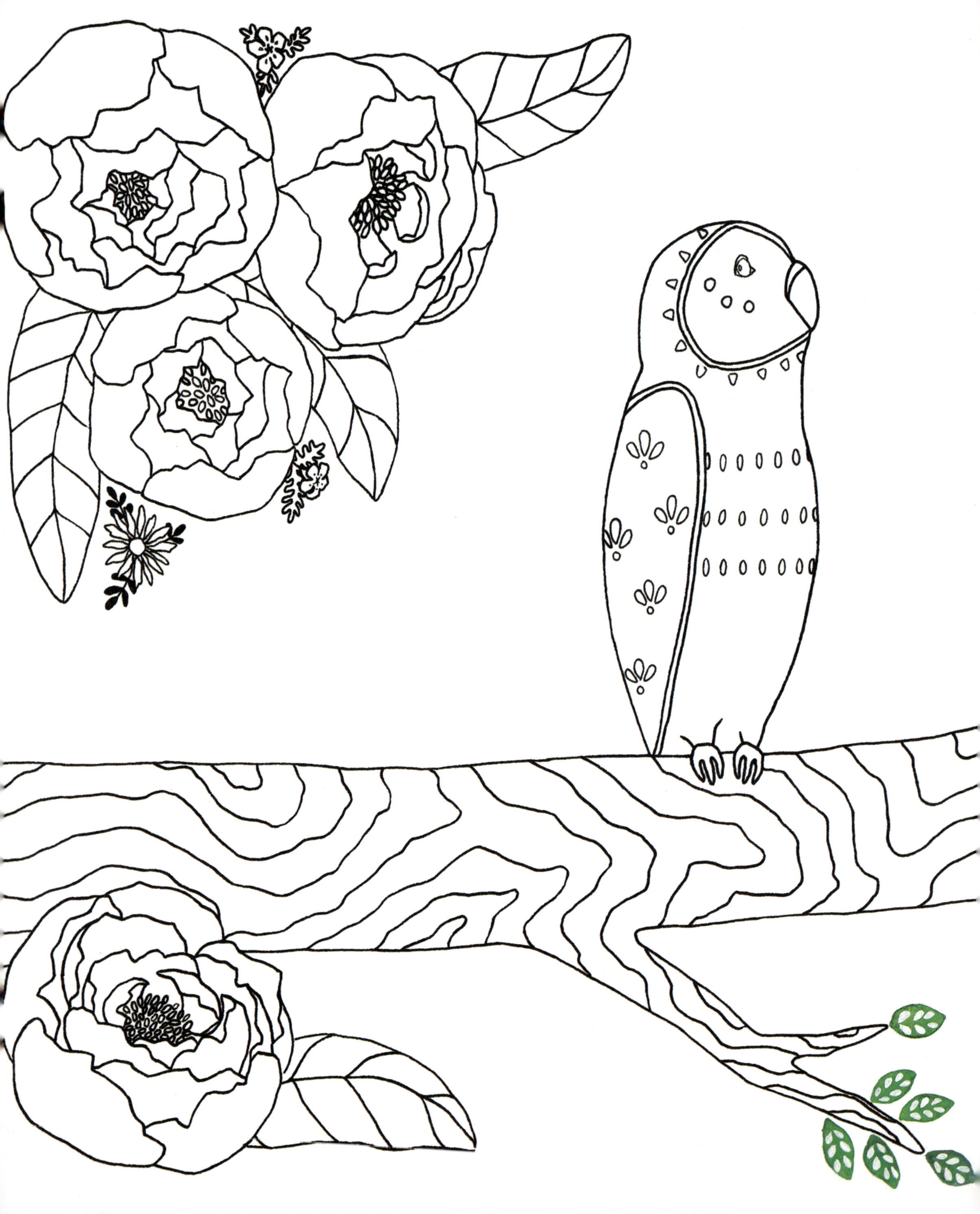

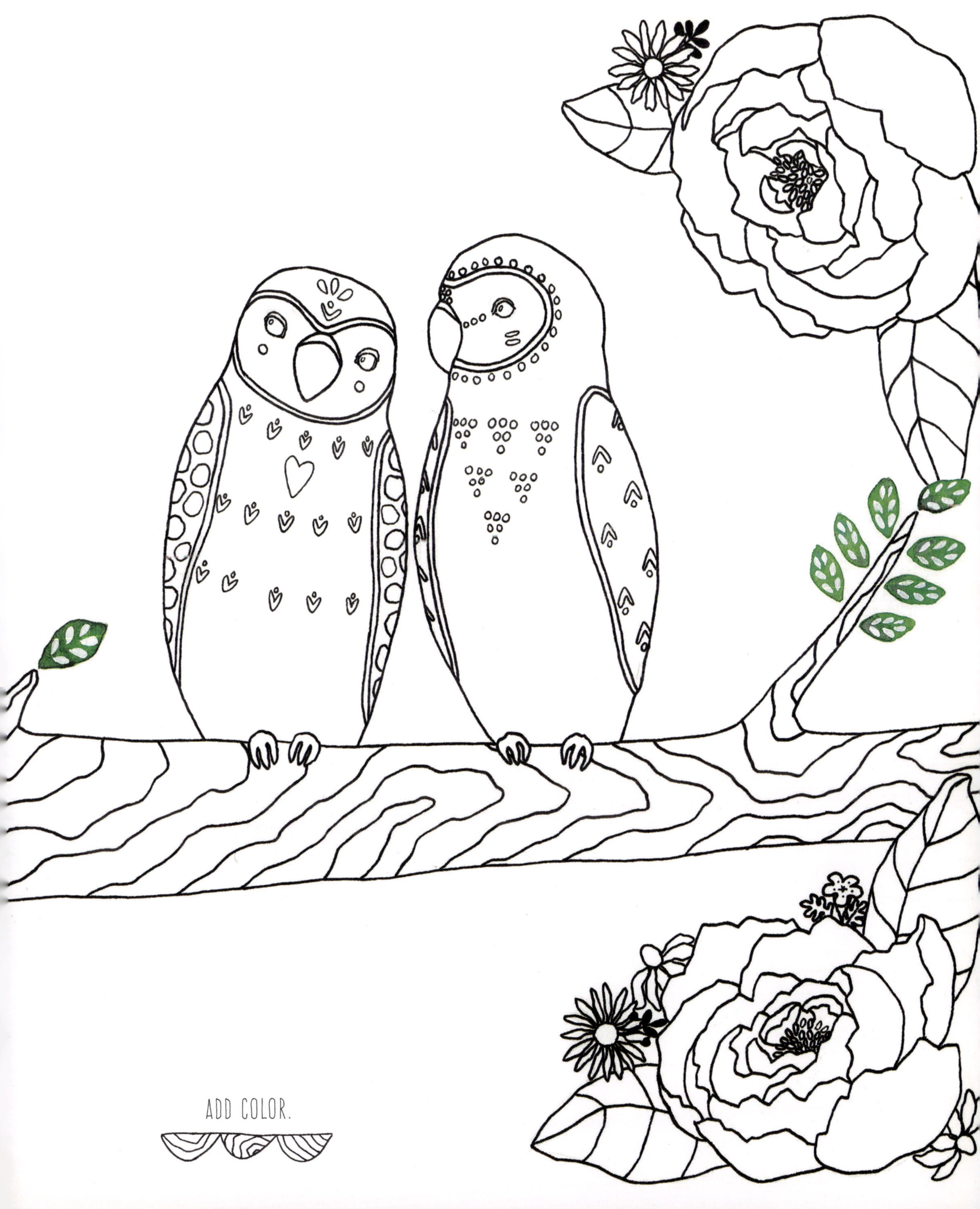
ADD COLOR.

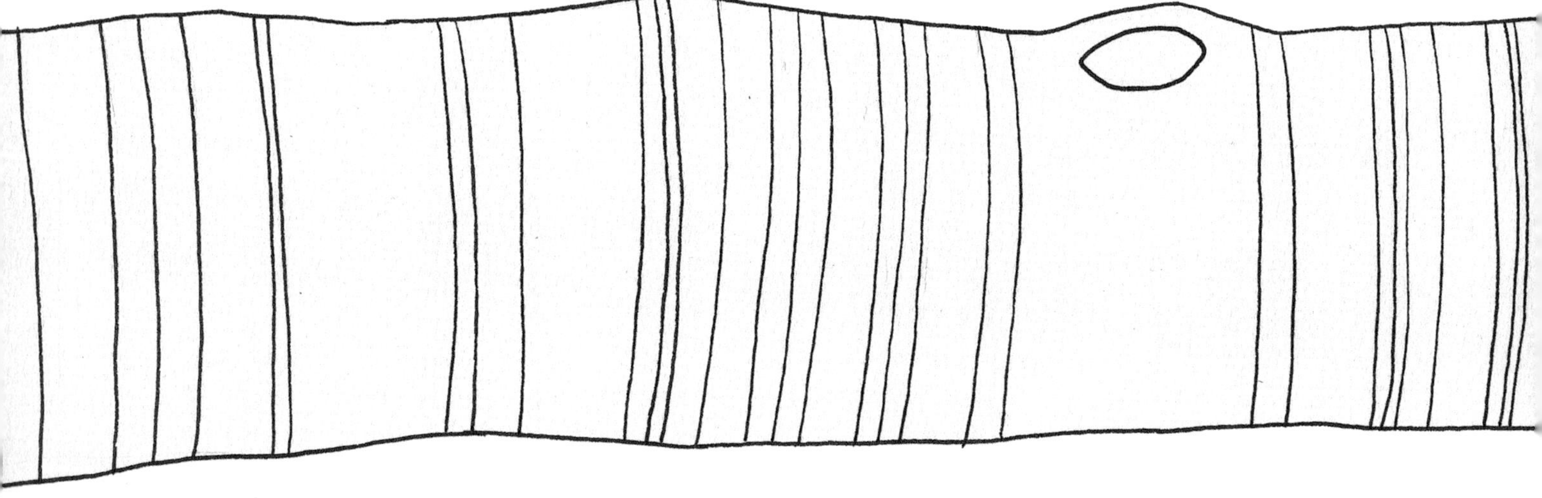

DRAW AND ADD LOVEBIRDS ON THE BRANCH.
CREATE THEIR WHIMSICAL SURROUNDINGS.

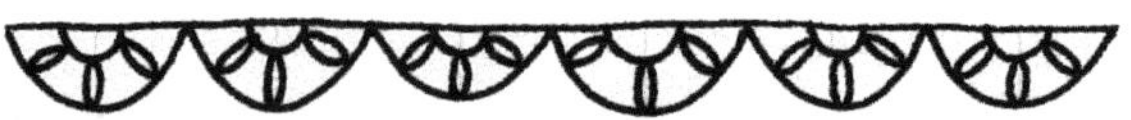

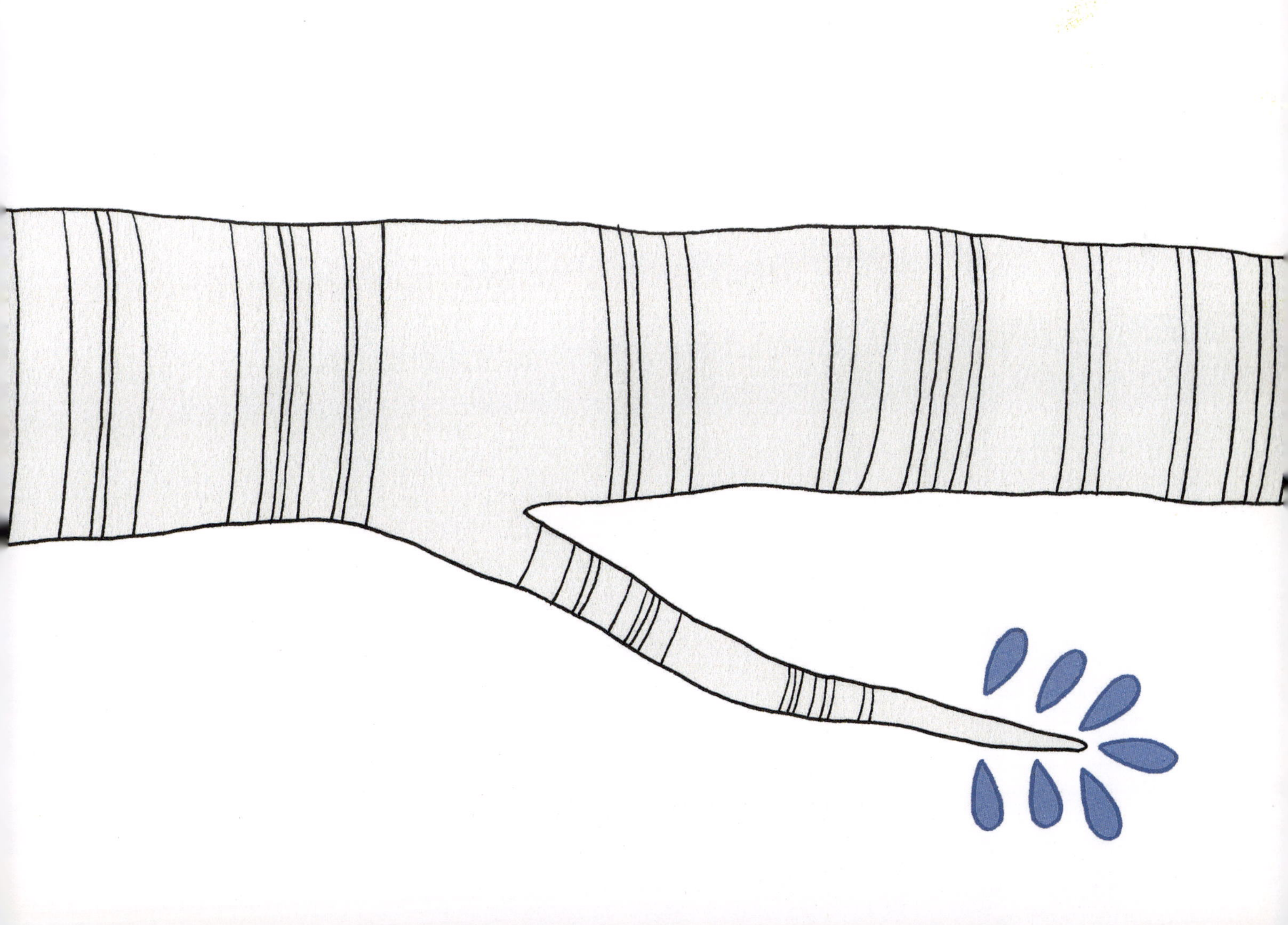

ABOUT THE ILLUSTRATOR

ARTIST AND ILLUSTRATOR MARISA REDONDO WORKS PRIMARILY WITH WATERCOLORS AND OILS. MOST OF HER WORK IS NATURE INSPIRED. ART HAS ALWAYS BEEN HER GREATEST LOVE. GROWING UP IN THE HEART OF SAN DIEGO, DRAWING WAS HOW SHE FOUND A CALM BALANCE IN THE BUSY CITY. CURRENTLY BASED IN NORTHERN CALIFORNIA, MARISA IS FASCINATED BY NATURE'S CREATIONS AND THE LITTLE PIECES OF LIFE THAT OFTEN GO UNNOTICED, FROM THE FINE LINES OF FEATHERS TO THE SPORES OF A DANDELION. THROUGH WATERCOLOR, SHE EXPLORES THE ORGANIC PATTERNS AND INTRICATE DETAILS IMPRESSED ON EVERYTHING FROM THE EARTH. HER PAINTINGS ARE A MIX OF THE MODERN CITY SHE CAME FROM AND THE NATURAL LAND WHERE SHE NOW LIVES.

LEARN MORE AT WWW.RIVERLUNAART.COM.

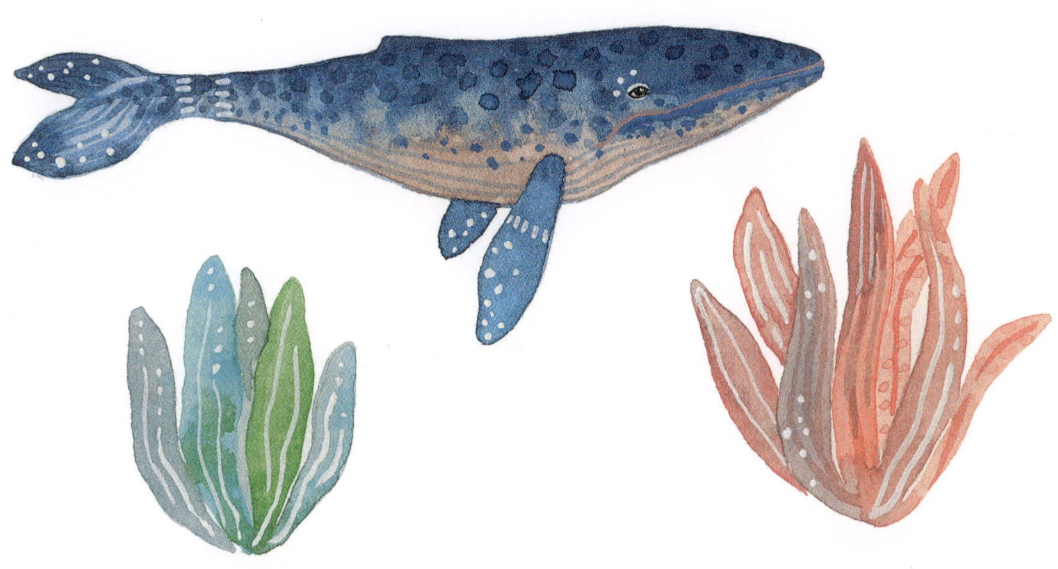

ALSO AVAILABLE

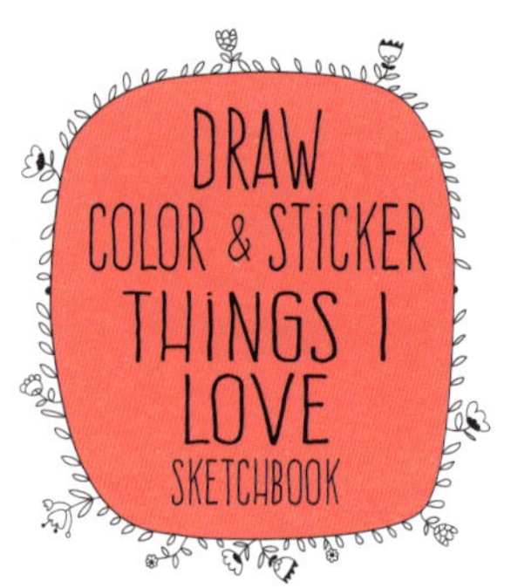

DRAW, COLOR, AND STICKER THINGS I LOVE SKETCHBOOK
978-1-63159-309-3

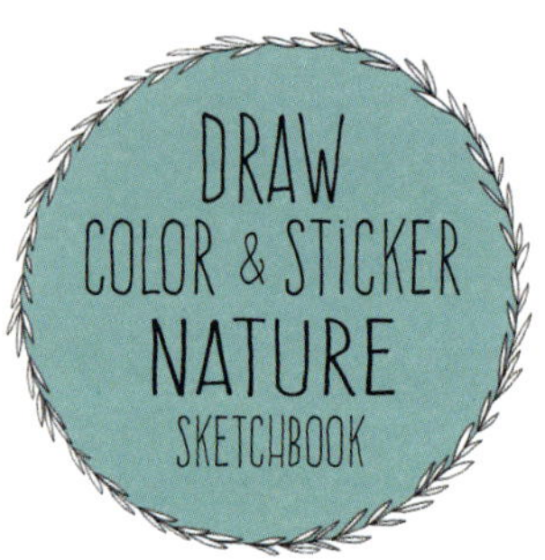

DRAW, COLOR, AND STICKER NATURE SKETCHBOOK
978-1-63159-278-2

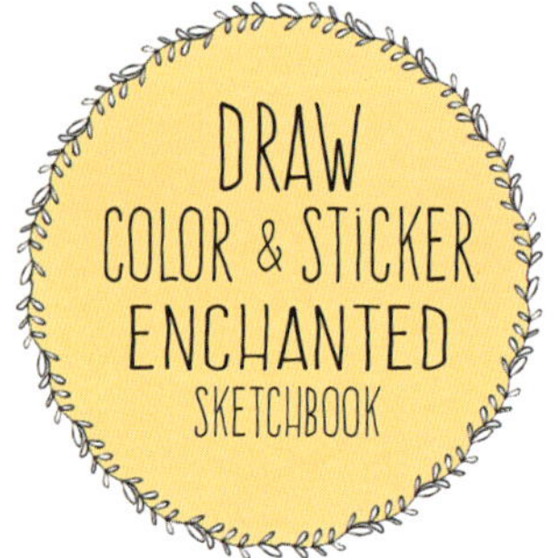

DRAW, COLOR, AND STICKER ENCHANTED SKETCHBOOK
978-1-63159-279-9

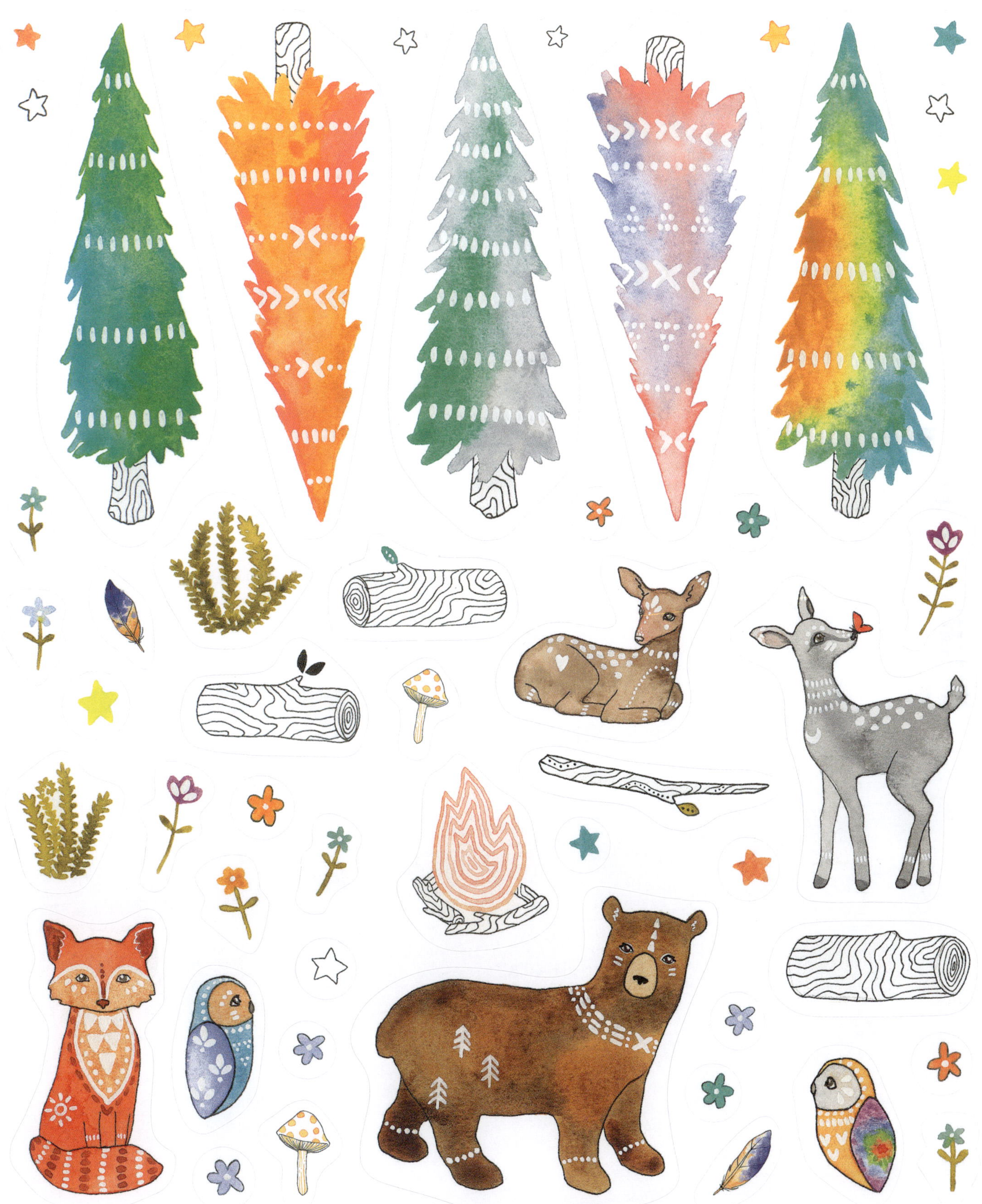
FOREST FRIENDS

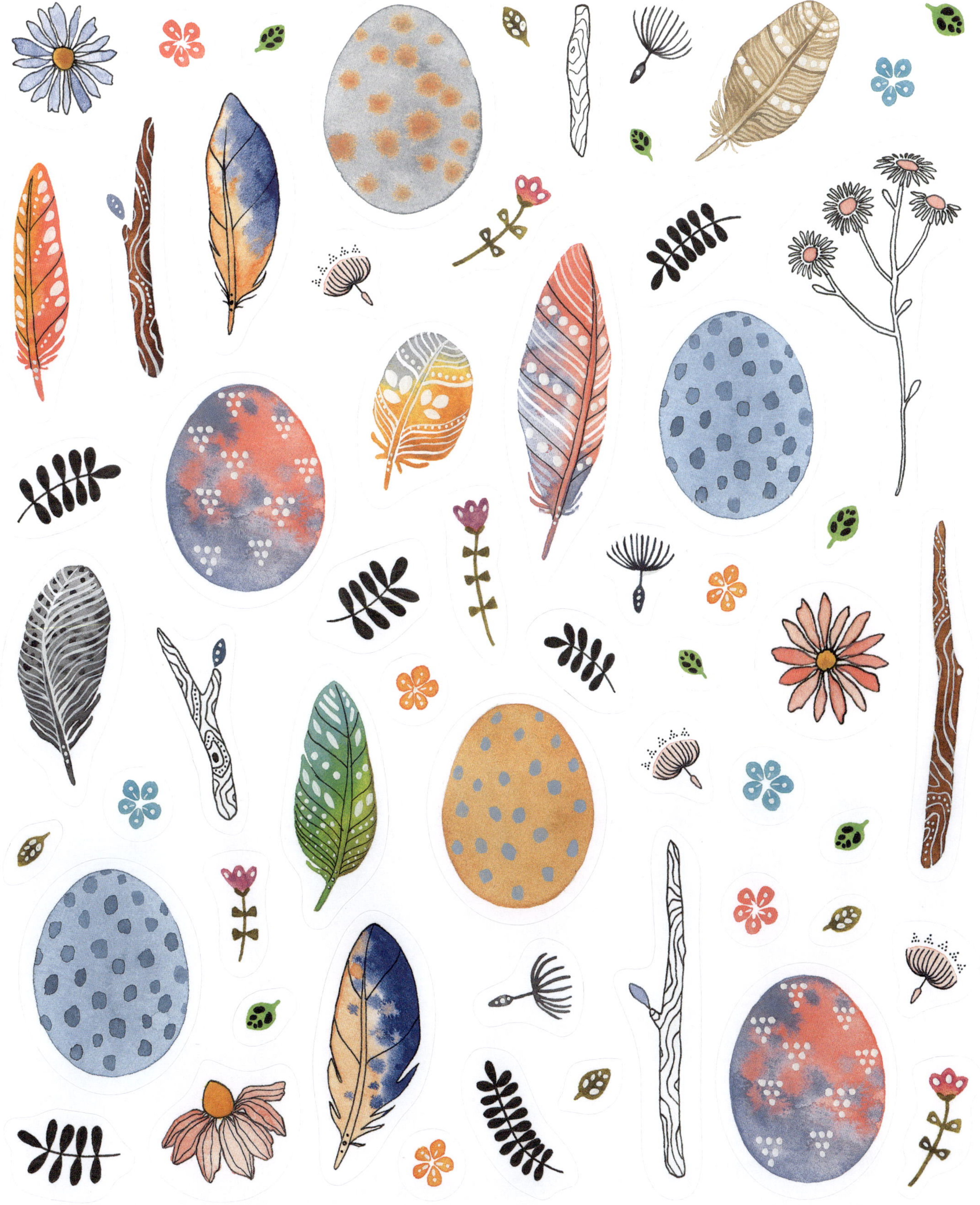

BIRD`S NEST

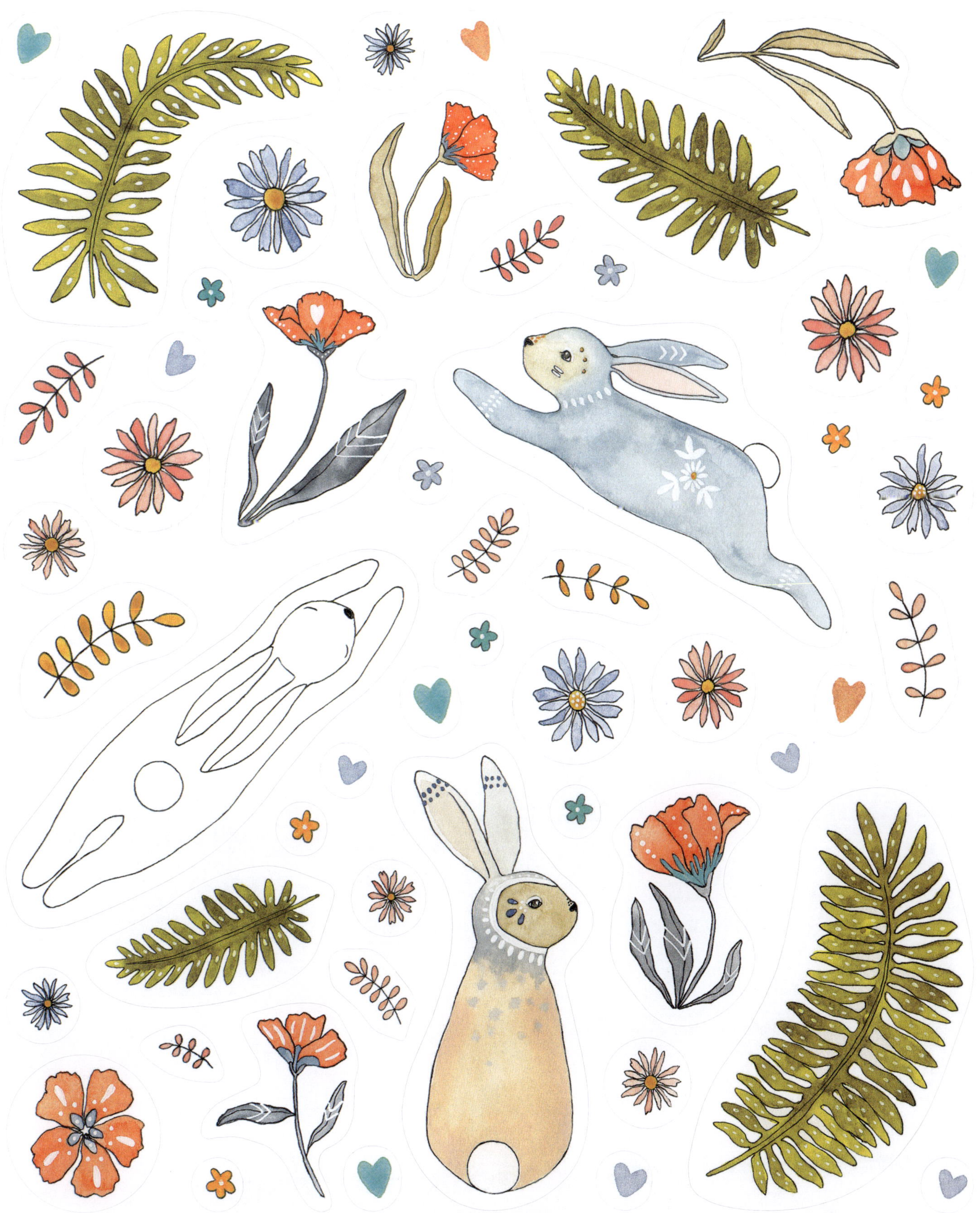

BUNNY MEADOW

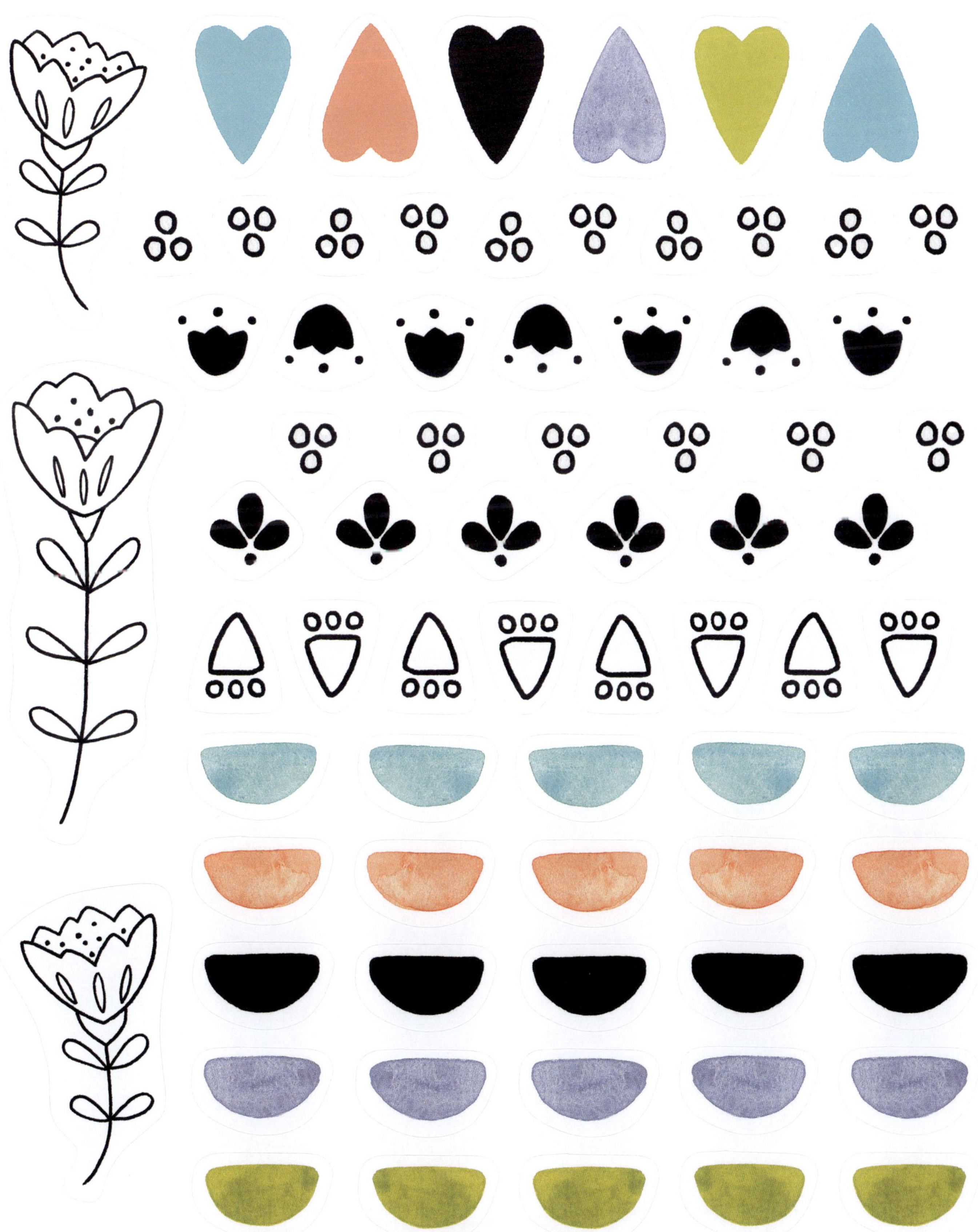

HONEY BEARS

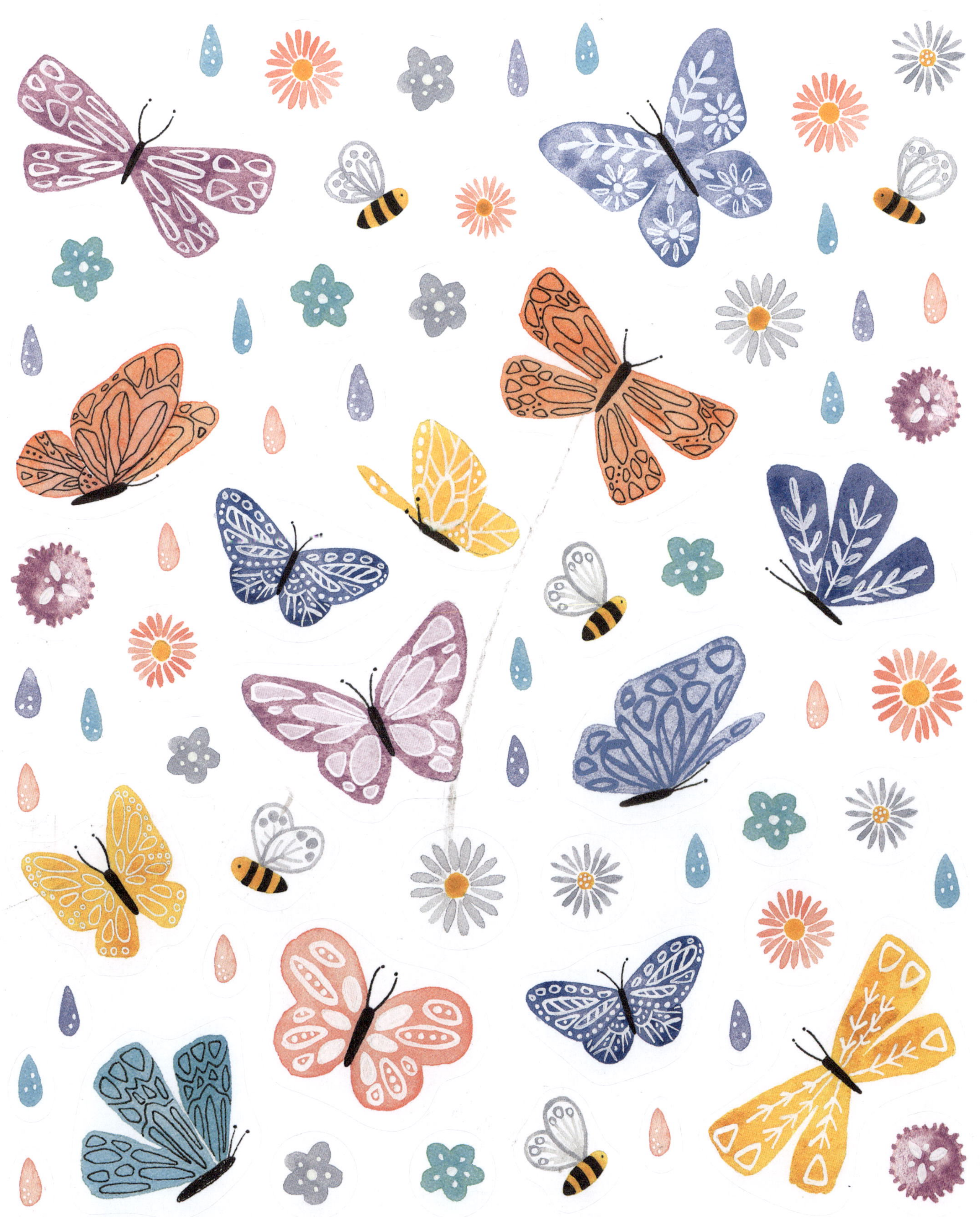

FLOWERS & BUTTERFLIES

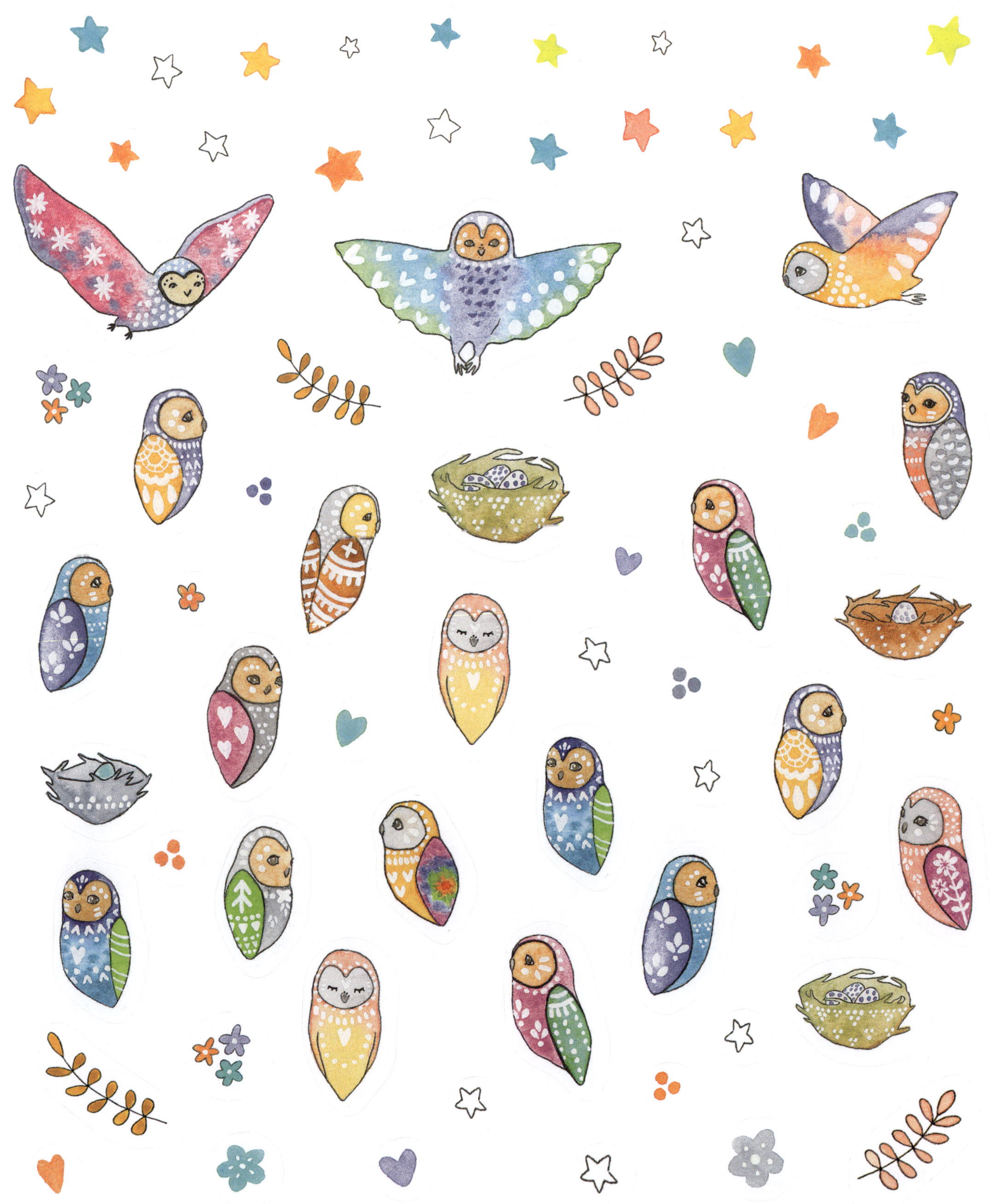

MIDNIGHT OWLS

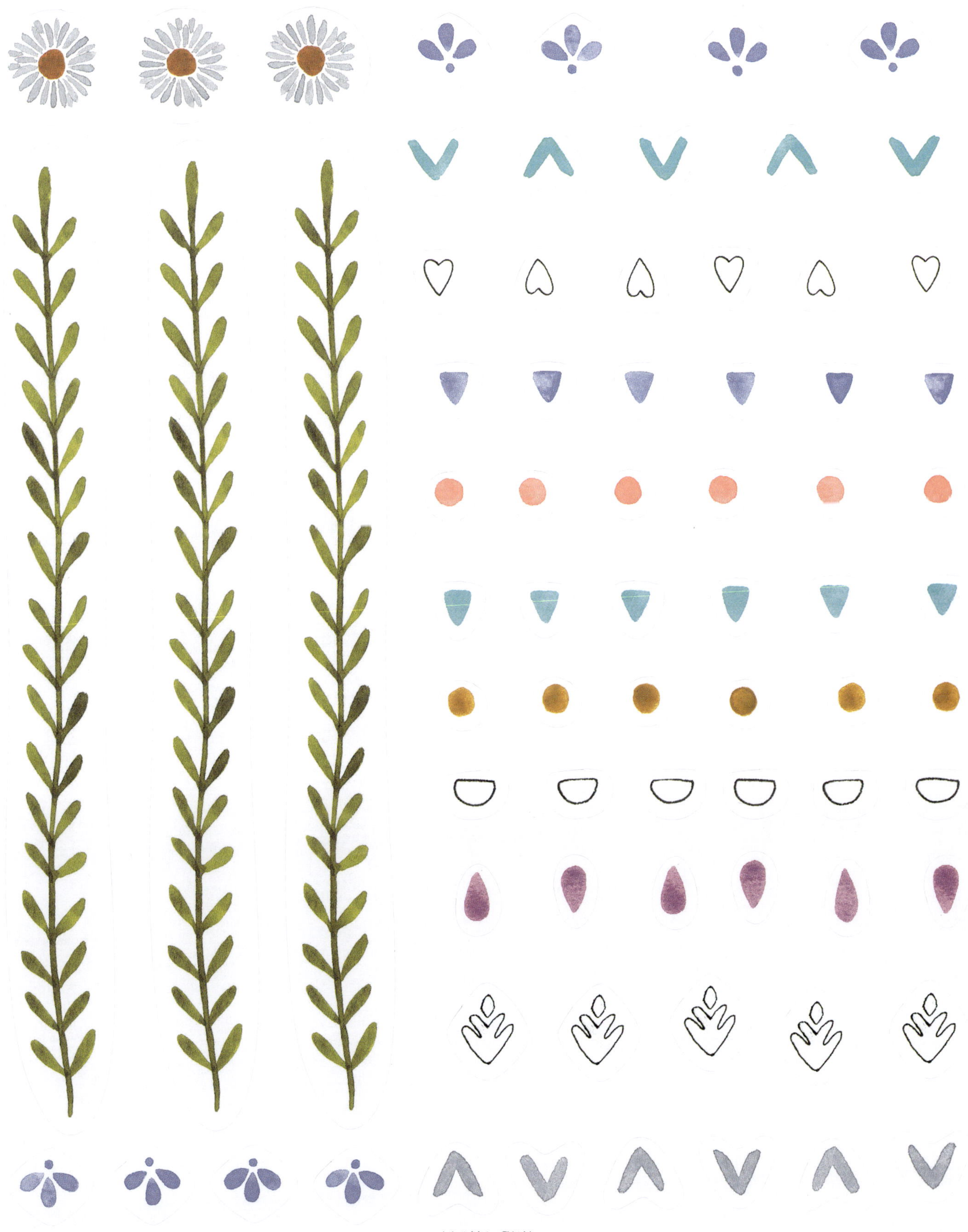

LLAMA FUN

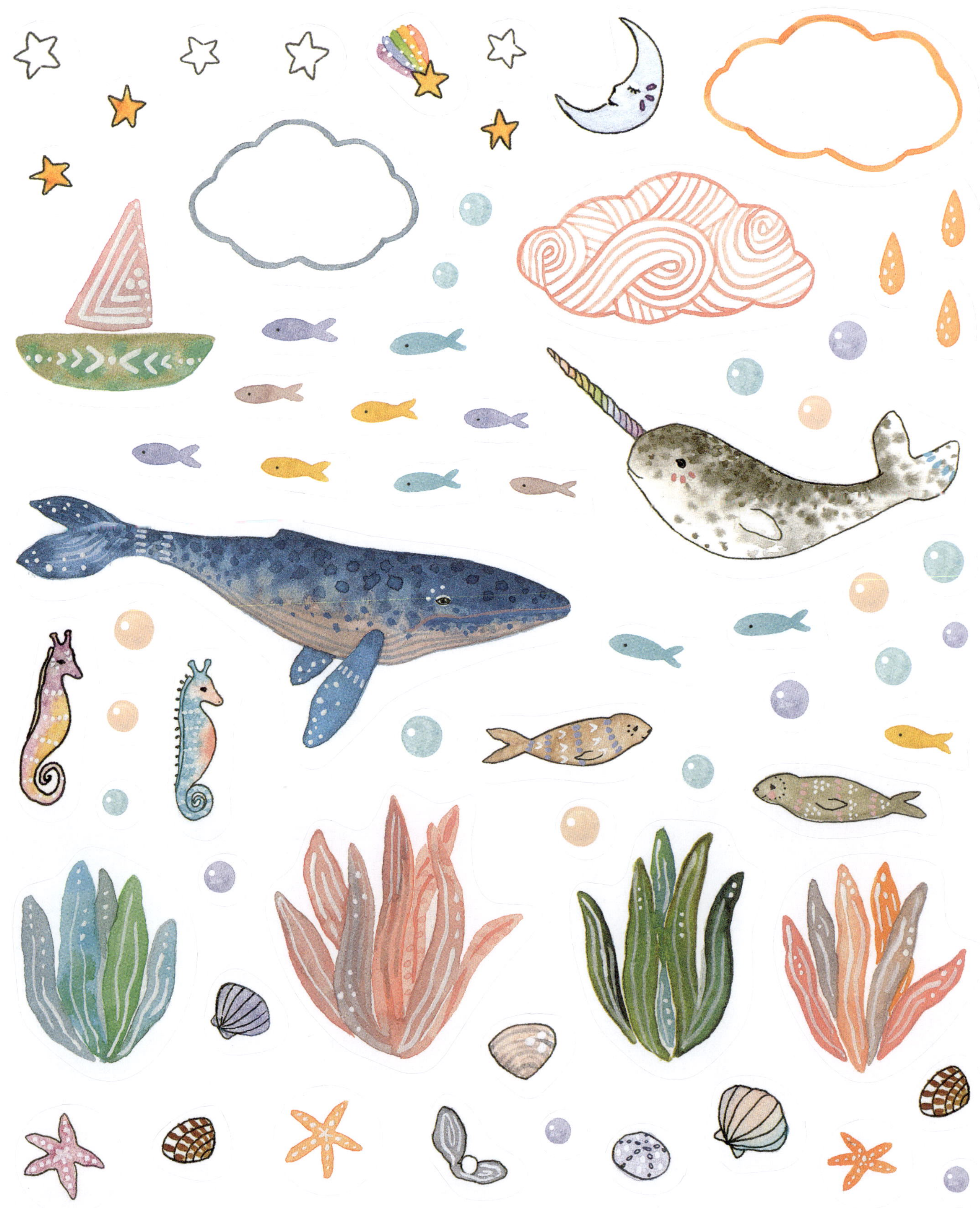

UNDER THE SEA

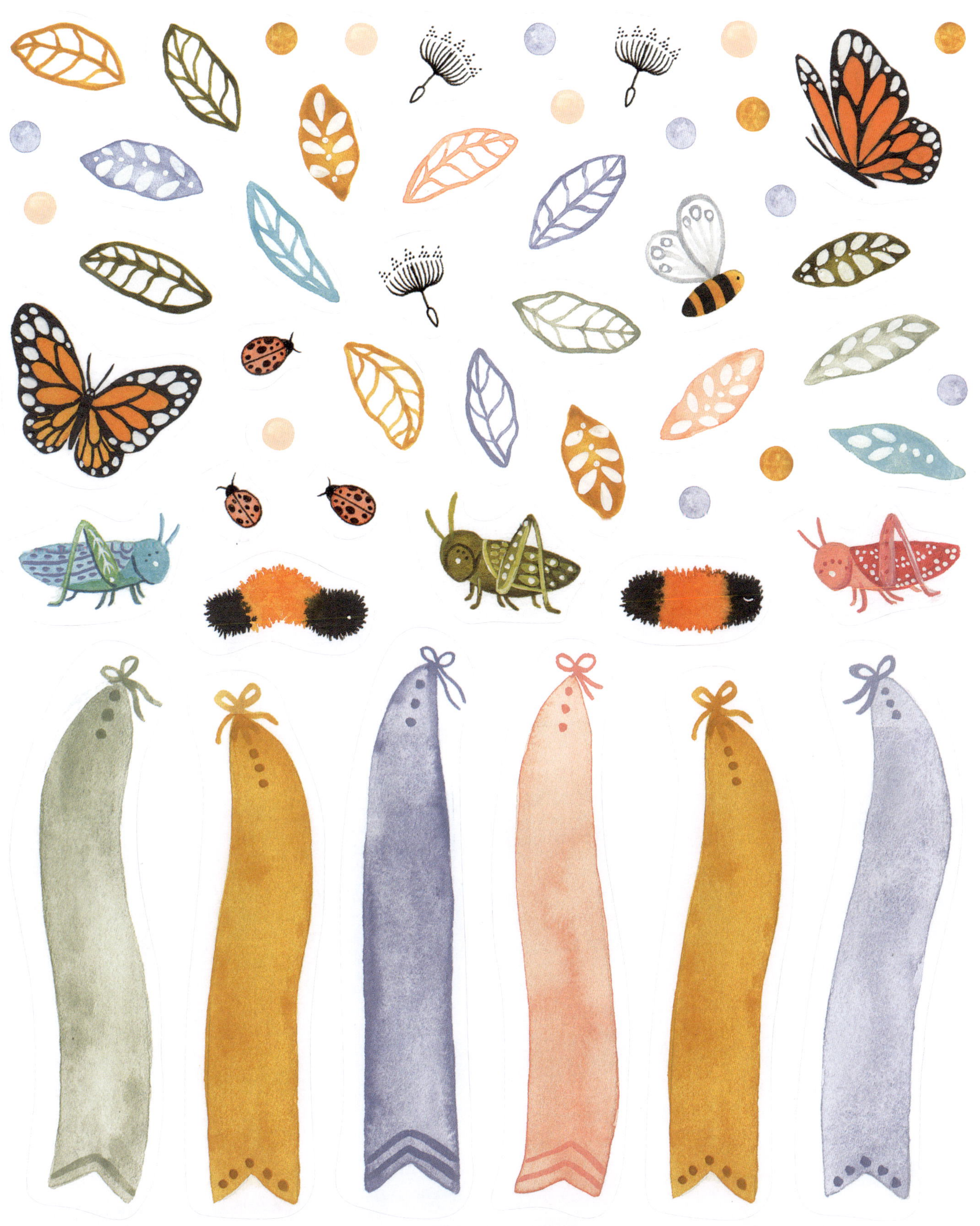
DANDELION WISHES

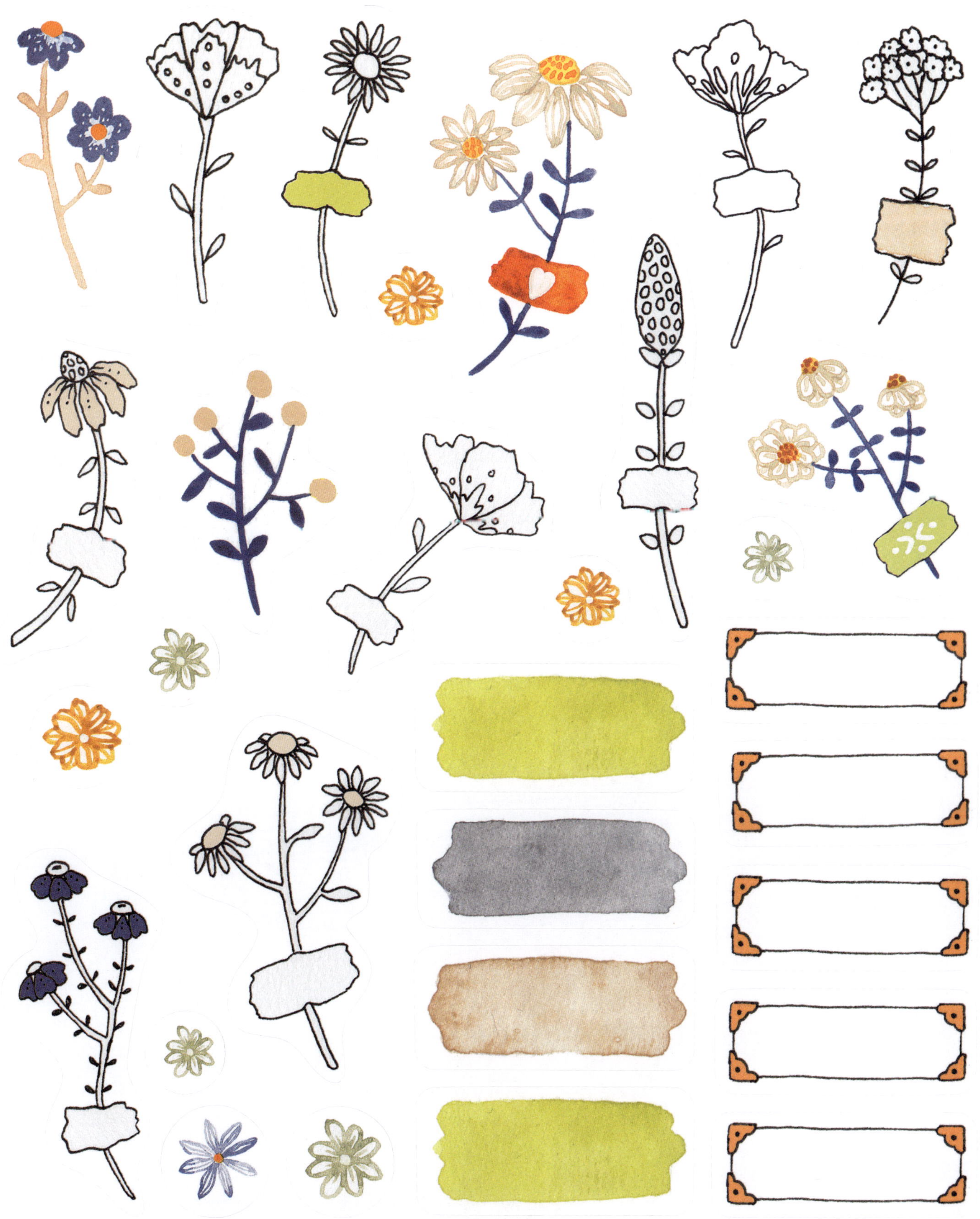

FLOWER PRESS

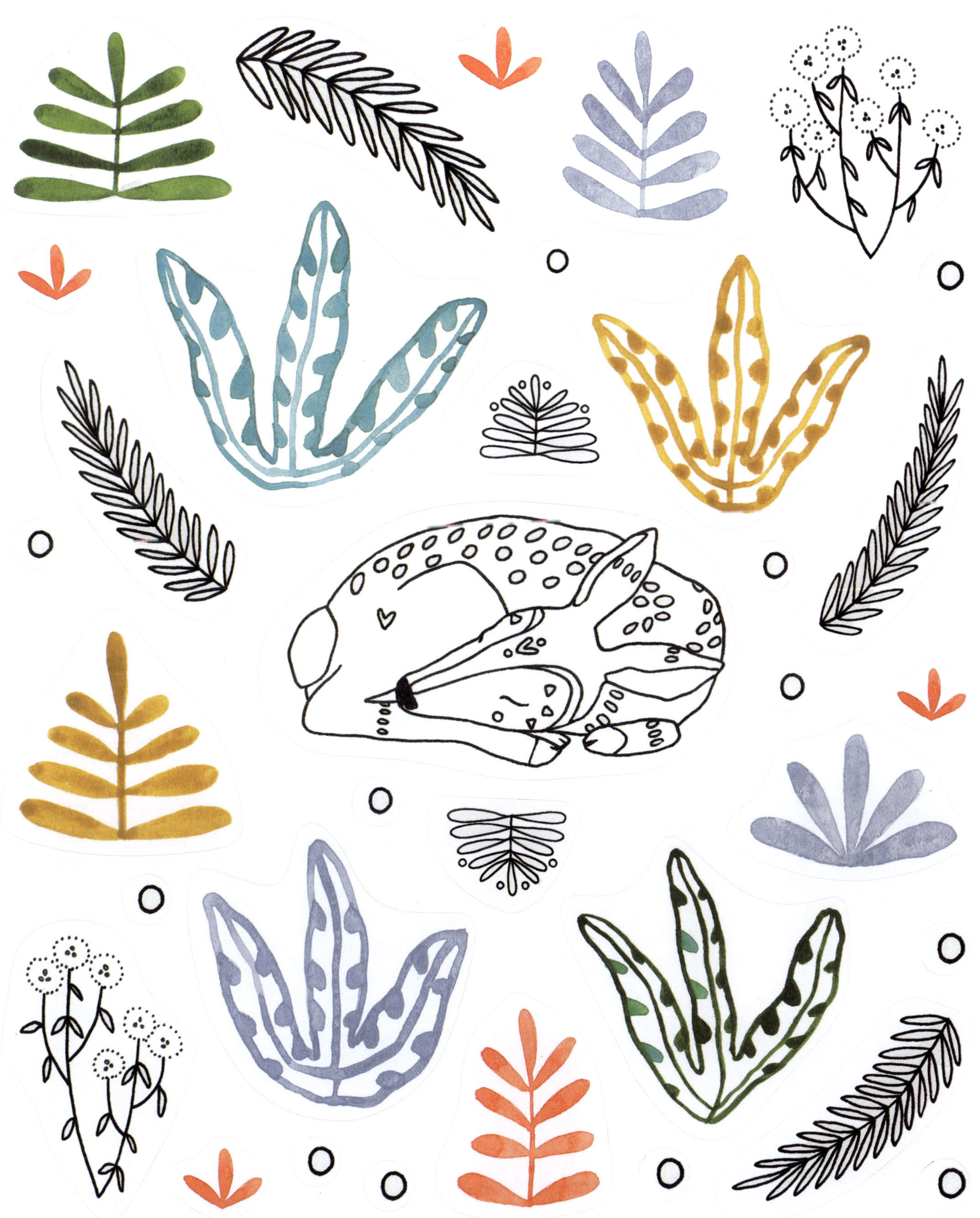

FAWN IN THE FOREST

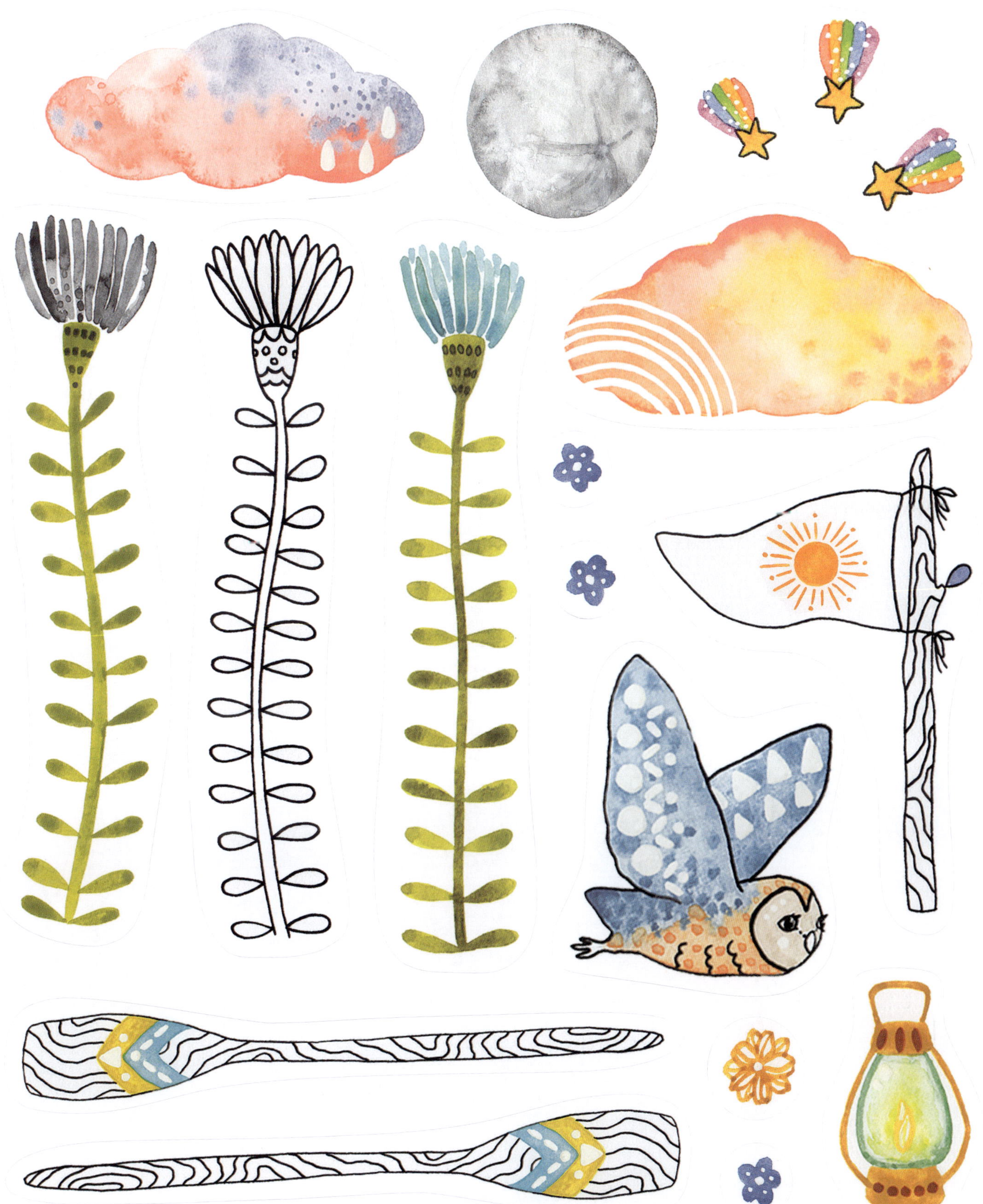

CANOE ADVENTURE

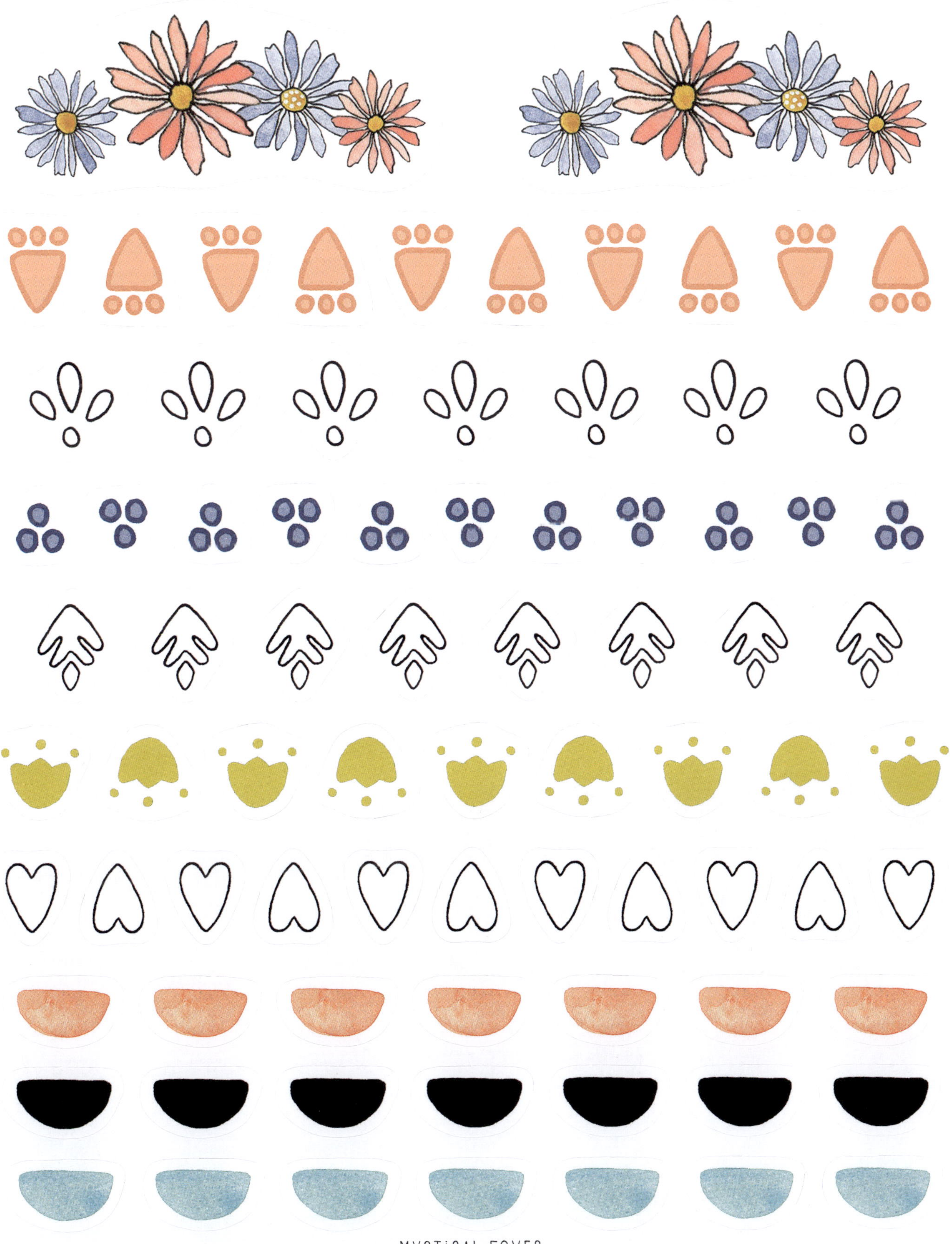

MYSTICAL FOXES

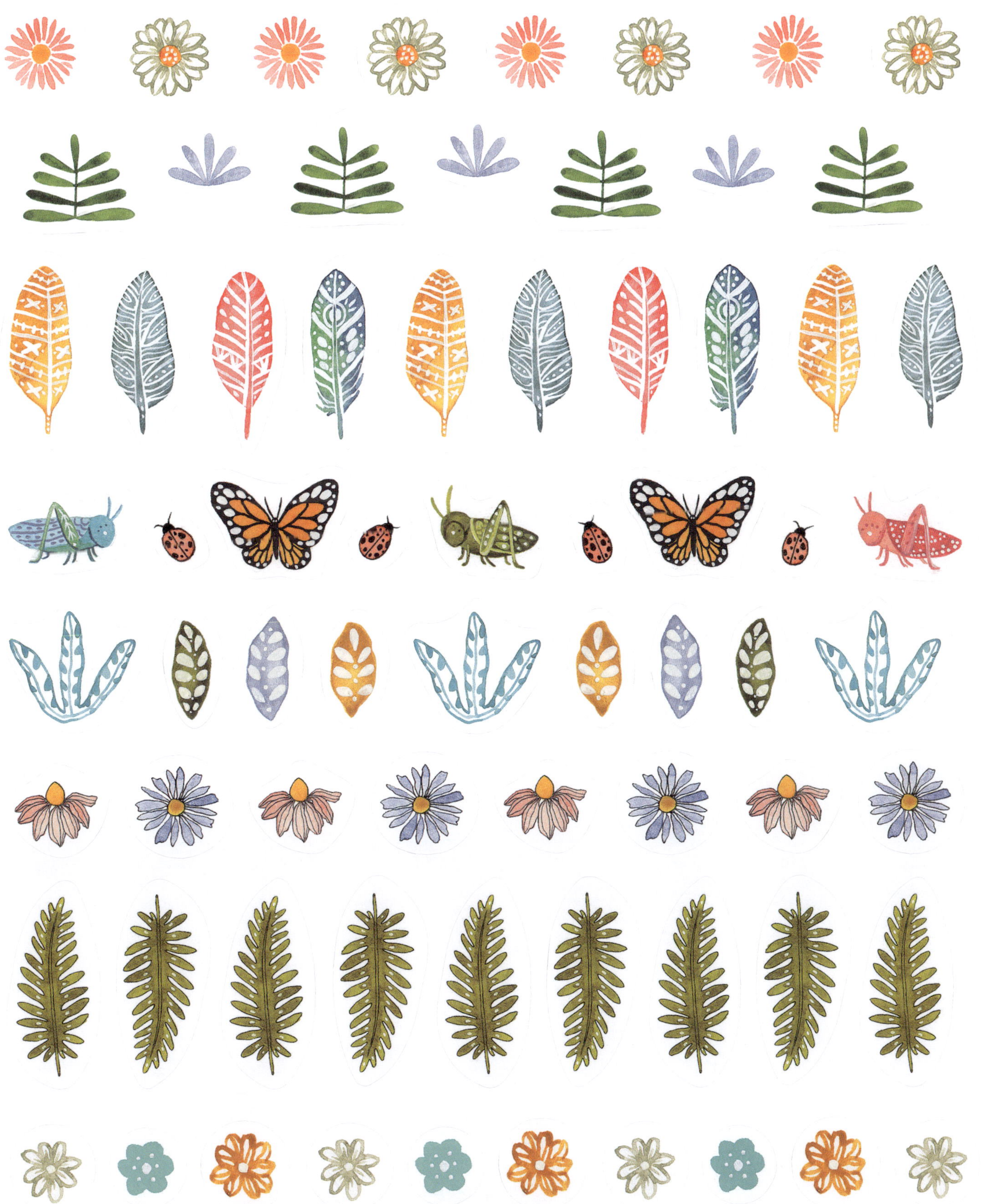

LOVEBIRDS

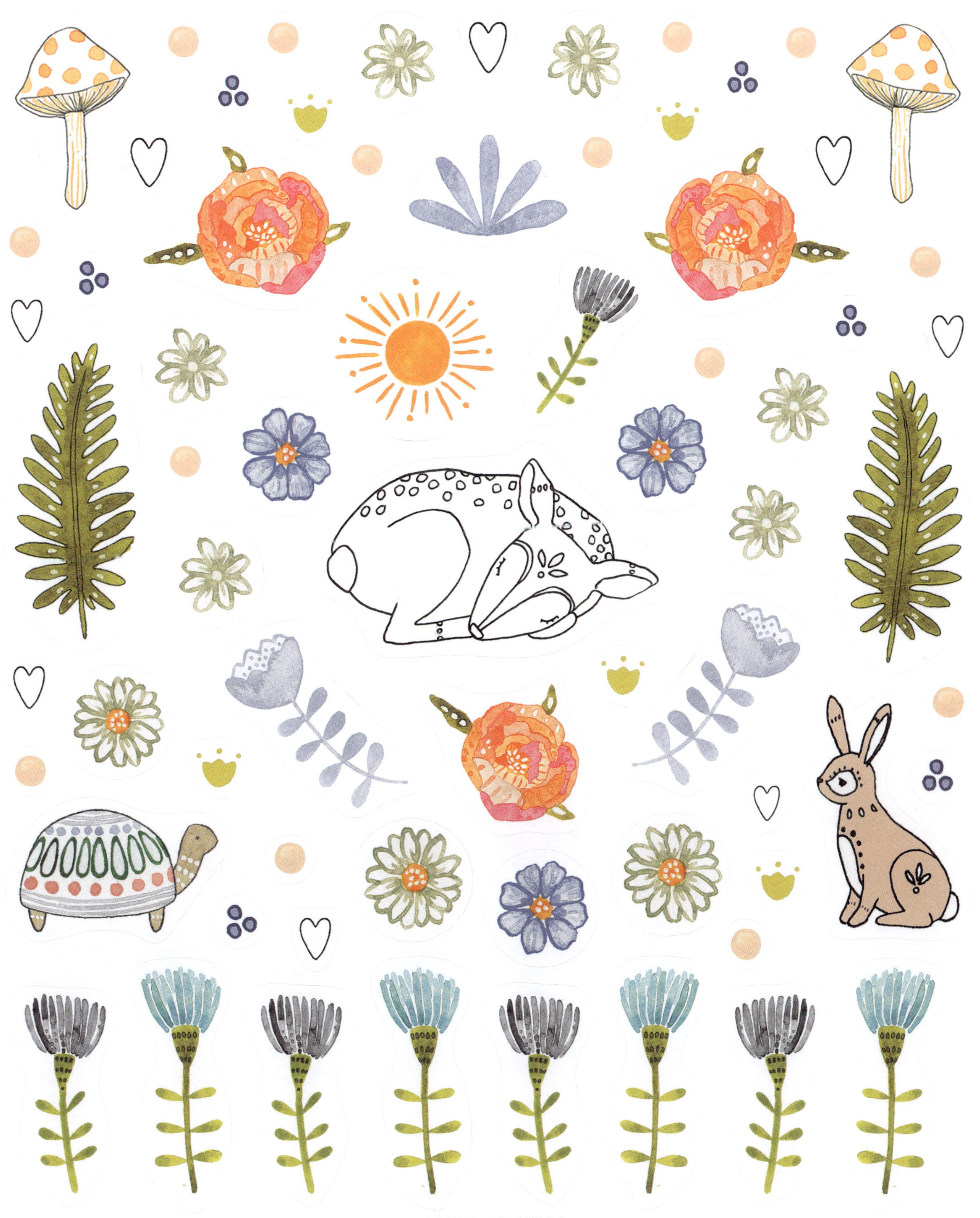

BONUS STICKERS

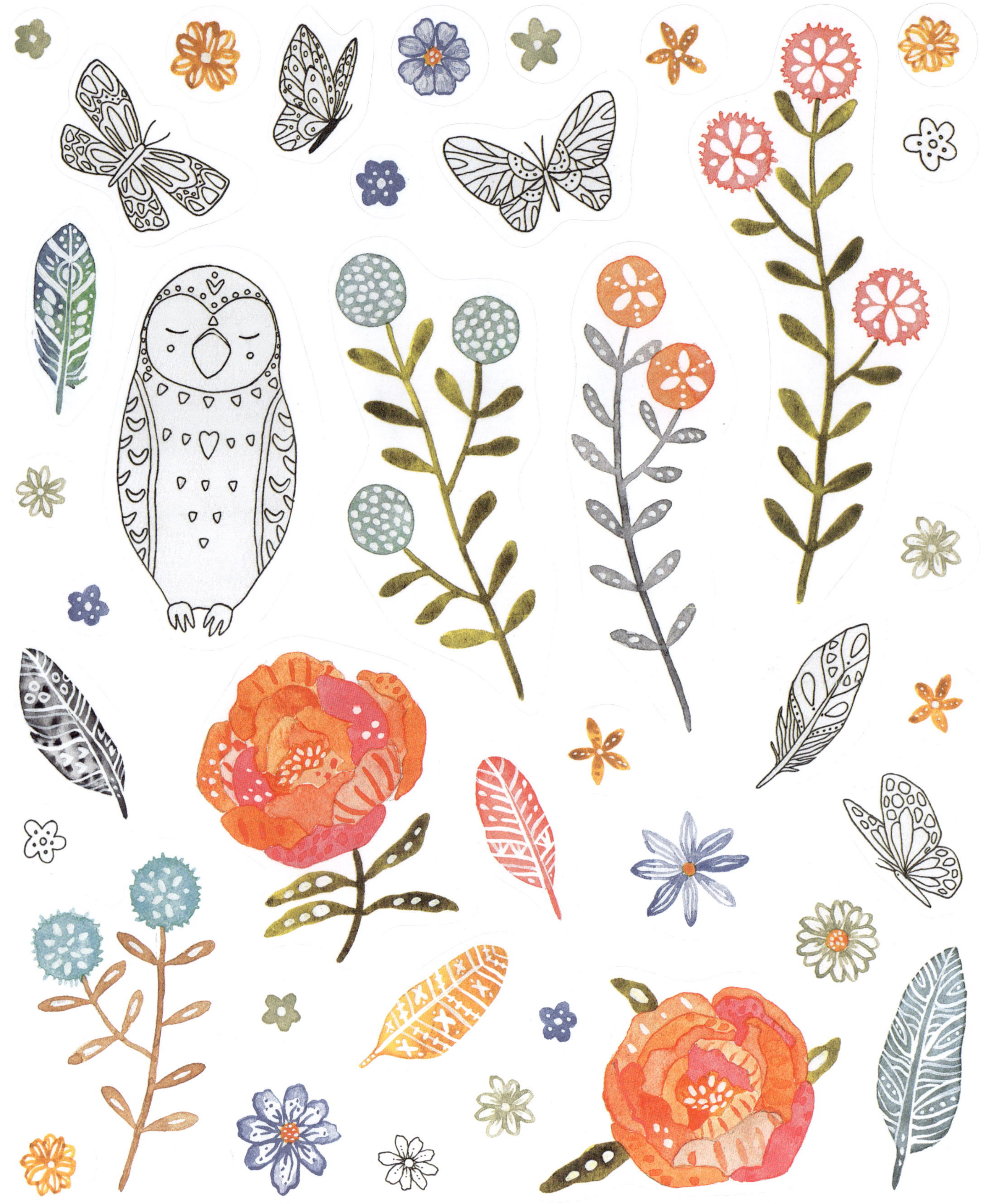